BEFORE YOU SAY I DO
AGAIN

A Buyer's Beware Guide to Remarriage

T0159043

Frederick Fell Publishers, Inc
2131 Hollywood Blvd., Suite 305
Hollywood, Fl 33020
www.Fellpub.com
email: Fellpub@aol.com

Frederick Fell Publishers, Inc
2131 Hollywood Blvd., Suite 305
Hollywood, Fl 33020

Copyright ©2009 by Benjamin H. Berkley. All rights reserved.

All rights reserved, including the right to reproduce this book or portions thereof in any form whatsoever, For information address to Frederick Fell Subsidiary Rights Department, 2131 Hollywood Boulevard, Suite 305, Hollywood, Florida 33020.

For information about special discounts for bulk purchases, Please contact Frederick Fell Special Sales at business@fellpub.com.

Designed by Elena Solis

Manufactured in the United States of America

10 9 8 7 6 5 4 3 2 1

Library of Congress Cataloging-in-Publication Data

Berkley, Benjamin.
 Before you say I do, again! / by Benjamin H. Berkley ; with "from the couch" client case analysis and a foreword by Denise Schieren.
    p. cm.
 ISBN 978-0-88391-173-0 (pbk. : alk. paper)
 1. Marriage law--United States--Popular works. 2. Remarriage--United States. I. Schieren, Denise. II. Title.
 KF510.Z9B47 2009
 346.7301'6--dc22

                                2009016147

ISBN 13: 978-0-88391-173-0

BEFORE YOU SAY I DO

A Buyer's Beware
Guide to Remarriage!

AGAIN

BENJAMIN H. BERKLEY

DEDICATION

"To Carl and Carolyn,
who certainly prove that a second marriage can bring
true love and happiness. Salud!"

ABOUT THE AUTHOR

Growing up in Long Beach, NY, young Ben Berkley was fascinated by daily black-and-white re-runs of the TV lawyer show Perry Mason. After getting a B.A. in Speech and Hearing from Adelphi University, in Garden City, N.Y., Berkley earned his legal degree from Western State University in Fullerton, CA. For the past 31 years he has conducted a busy general practice which includes divorce, estate planning, family law, social security disability appeals and bankruptcy. During the past three years he has also served as Judge Pro Tem for the Orange County Superior Court. His previous books are: My Wishes: Your Plan for Organizing and Communicating Your Family's Needs; The Complete Executor's Guide and Winning Your Social Security Disability Case.

PREFACE

"I just hope I don't make the same mistake twice."

Believe it or not, this is the phrase most often spoken by a client at the end of a divorce hearing. But regardless of the destruction a marital breakup can cause, as well as the emotional pain that is often not limited to the parties getting divorced, with the passing of time most divorcees decide they wish to give love another try. Statistically speaking, more than seventy percent of persons who divorce do remarry eventually.

For many, remarriage does offer a second chance at love and to live happily ever after. But for those not so lucky souls, a second marriage often ends sooner than the first and can prove to be far more painful. Why is this so? Well perhaps because you've been down that road before, there is a false sense of security in believing that the second time around is going to be easier than the first. However, tying the knot again is not like repeating Biology in college with the hope of getting a higher grade. In fact, having a prior marriage may actually hurt your chances of success the second time around as second weddings have their own unique challenges.

In writing this book, it is not my intention to frighten you into believing that every man or woman out there is wrong for you. On the contrary! Marriage is still viewed as a wonderful institution and most people agree they would rather be married than single. I am certainly not suggesting that you have to kiss dozens of frogs before you meet your Prince Charming or Princess Bride. He or she is out there patiently waiting to meet you. You just need to learn how to distinguish the frogs from royalty.

SETTING THE RECORD STRAIGHT, WHAT THIS BOOK IS NOT

This is not a wedding planning book. There will be plenty of time to select where you will be married, order the invitations, choose your wedding cake, and begin dreaming about your honeymoon.

Think of this book as your insurance policy; if you're wise enough to follow the advice being given, you can count on celebrating many wedding anniversaries in the years to come following the big day!

TABLE OF CONTENTS

Foreword By Denise Schieren, PsyD.

When a marriage begins to falter, between the he said and she said, lies the truth of what is going wrong and needs to be corrected. However, instead of uncovering the problem and working together to resolve it, first time married couples often make a mad dash for divorce court when they should be heading to the marriage counselor's office.

As a result, issues which led to the initial breakup remain unaddressed and unresolved. Then out of the blue, you meet someone new. The relationship is exciting and your past failure starts to fade and becomes a distant memory. You and your new love interest are moving forward and there is talk about getting married. Wedding plans are made but what went wrong in your first marriage is now overshadowed by the thought of walking down the aisle again.

So begins a typical remarriage with all its bumps and grinds. And though many couples learn to work through it, for the majority of those who have been married before, remarriage presents daily challenges that often threaten to weaken the relationship. Failing to recognize what went wrong the first time increases the odds that the second marriage is also destined to go down in flames.

In counseling couples where one or both spouses have had prior marriages, ironically what I have often found is the problems they experienced during their first marriage are the same ones they are dealing with now. It seems the only thing that has changed is the year and names on the calendar. But unlike first time married individuals who sooner opt for divorce rather than attempting counseling, persons who have remarried express to me that they see themselves as potentially failing at love the second time around. They are trying to avoid becoming a part of that overwhelming statistic of failed second marriages having long ago realized that love alone will not guarantee everything will work out.

Before the invitations are sent out, the flowers ordered, and the champagne toast is given, Before You Say I Do, Again, will open your eyes as to what went wrong the first time, not to mention provide you with all the necessary knowledge you'll need to know before you say I do, again. Written from the viewpoint of an attorney who has dealt with divorce proceedings more than he'd care to admit, it is your prescription to marital health.

INTRODUCTION

WARNING LABEL: This book may cause anxiety. It is best read when consuming ice cream, chocolate, or alcohol. If you are starting a new relationship, this book should be read once a day. If you are engaged, it should be read four times a day. Regardless, always consult your attorney if you feel an uncontrollable urge to get remarried.

Learning from the mistakes of a failed first marriage and telling yourself you will do better the next time around is like saying if you've lost a football game you'll win the next one. You will but only if you learn some new plays before getting back on the field. As an attorney, I have seen all the warning signs and Before You Say I Do, Again! will teach you those new plays to avoid coming up on the losing side again.

When you married the first time, you thought you knew everything there was to know about that person. Unfortunately, having lived through a failed marriage, you have also learned there were a lot of things you didn't know before having said I do. Even though you are now older and wiser, this does not necessarily guarantee you will not make the same mistakes again. This is precisely the reason I chose to write this book.

Having practiced law for more than thirty years, I have seen hundreds of cases concerning all issues of family law. A significant number of these cases involved second marriages. During the initial consultation, clients often feel this is the time to vent about their Soon-To-Be-Ex. They also take a retrospective look at themselves and candidly discuss the mistakes they've made in the past. In preparation for this book, I have chronicled this information, as well as conducted countless interviews with former clients.

Second time brides and grooms may think they know more the second time around but statistics prove they don't. For first marriages, one out of every two can be expected to end in tears.(,_) And if our optimism steers us into marriage, it goes into overdrive with remarriage. Despite the disappointment, pain, disruption, and sometimes even the destruction of a first divorce, most of us opt to get back on the horse as an astonishing seventy percent of the broken-hearted get married all over again.

Yet, according to a study conducted by Psychology Today, a whopping sixty percent of remarriages fail. They do so at a much faster rate than first marriages with the greatest risk of divorce existing when one or both spouses have children from a previous marriage. Furthermore, experience doesn't count when it comes to remarriage as a prior marriage actually decreases the odds of a second union working out.

In navigating the often choppy seas of remarriage, it is all too common to be blinded by the excitement of remarriage. As a result, it is much too easy to steer off course. With stories retold from clients of their experiences, and with a sprinkling of humor added to keep your sanity, Before You Say I Do, Again! will alert you to the obvious and not so obvious warning signs that are often ignored along the path of remarriage. It will also explain why character wins out over personality, as well as illustrate how compatibility may be even more sensuous than chemistry.

For instance, many of my clients have expressed that they see themselves as a loser; lost in love and in marriage. It is a true statement that a marriage ending in divorce is a failure. However, the crux of the matter is there were reasons why the marriage failed and it would be unfair to you to put total blame on yourself. It is also not healthy to dwell on what you did wrong as that marriage is behind you now. You have a full life ahead of you and deserve to find happiness. Likewise, you have something wonderful to offer another human being and deserve to find someone who can reciprocate this same kind of warmth.. This book will help you spend your time learning how to get love and marriage right the second time around.

In addition, with second marriages, there is more at stake. Chances are one or both of you have accumulated assets and the book will offer a discussion of how to legally protect them and shall include sample forms including prenuptial and postnuptial agreements.

Before You Say I Do, Again! will also raise issues that are not romantic but must be addressed. To illustrate, does he have debts that will now become "our" responsibility? What will be your legal responsibility? Are there health concerns? Will her kids ever like you? Or though the age difference doesn't seem like a big deal now, will you still feel the same way about him in fifteen years?

The book also presents the questions you must ask yourself before you walk down the aisle again. Such as:

- Why did I get married before?
- Was I really in love with my first wife/husband?
- Did I like him/her?
- Why did my marriage fail?
- How did I contribute to the destruction of the relationship?
- How is my remarriage going to change?

In addition, many of the chapters will include probing questions you should ask the person you intend to marry. Please be advised, there is no answer key in the back of the book revealing right or wrong answeres, so cheating your way through a second marriage is not a viable option..Instead, you are going to be the designated grader and whether your future spouse passes or fails will ultimately be decided by you.

Finally, Before You Say I Do, Again!, is an instructional guide for anyone who is considering tying the knot again. Regardless of whether your first marriage ended peacefully with little bruises or was an emotional nightmare that has left you scarred for life, this book will guide you through all the steps you'll need to take before stepping up to the altar.

Note, solely for convenience and to avoid confusion, I have chosen the female gender when referring to him or her. However, the material is equally applicable to both sexes.

THE BOOK IS DIVIDED INTO FOUR PARTS:

PART ONE is titled Navigating the Sea of Divorce (Do You Really Want to Jump Back in the Water?) and it takes you back in time to what may be an unpleasant revisit of your life when you were married and why you are now single. It will remind you of the displeasing sounds of divorce that are often forgotten when one considers getting hitched again.

PART TWO discusses what you will need to do before *Getting Ready to Say I Do, Again!* This includes becoming emotionally, financially, and legally ready to enter into yet another marriage. At the end of Part Two is a test for you to take that will help determine if you are prepared to say I do, again.

PART THREE is appropriately named Kick the Tires and Check Under the Hood, as I take the same approach to remarriage as buying a car; there is a great deal more you need to know that you may not have discovered the first time you said I do.

PART FOUR is a compatibility test to determine how your new partner compares with your former spouse. While you may be looking for someone who is the complete opposite of him or her, the results may surprise you.

Once you determine that all systems are go, Appendix A-C provides useful forms to protect you in case your remarried life is not exactly the fairytale ending you hoped it would be. Forms found in this section include:

- A Last Will and Testament with a guardianship provision
- Pre-Nuptial Agreement
- Asset Organizer

Finally, in anticipation of your nuptials, let me be the first to raise my flute glass high in the air and wish you both a very happy, healthy, and prosperous re-marriage.

Cheers.
Ben Berkley

PART ONE

NAVIGATING THE SEA OF DIVORCE:
(DO YOU REALLY WANT
TO JUMP BACK IN THE WATER?)

Ch 1

SHOULD I OPEN A RESTAURANT OR REMARRY?
BEATING THE ODDS AGAINST
A SUCCESSFUL REMARRIAGE

Q: Why do divorced men get married again?
A: Bad memory

As a kid, I loved to ride my bicycle. I liked to ride it as fast as my legs could peddle. But because of my reckless riding, I broke my arm four times when I fell off my bike.. With such a bad history of injuries and pain, you would think that I would've learned to be more careful. NOPE. Each time the cast came off, I got back on my bike. The only reason I probably did not break my arm more than four times is that when I turned sixteen I got my driver's license. Since then, I have been a safe driver and have never fallen out of my car.

The same comparison to falling off my bike and getting back on can be made to remarriage. Just because you were married before does not necessarily make you any smarter going into a second marriage. Statistics bear this out as more than seventy percent of persons who didn't get it right the first time around remarry again. Of this group, however, over sixty percent go their separate ways before death do they part. Even more alarming, the length of the second marriage is usually even shorter than the first.

So, with all the horrible statistics that point to a failed remarriage, why do so many opt to say I do, again? Is it because we believe that true happiness can only be found through marriage? Or do we simply not want to die alone? Perhaps it is because we see ourselves as the baseball pitcher who lost the big game and wants to prove to the world that he can still be a winner. Perhaps it is because people are too anxious to get back on the bike only to suffer the pain of falling off all over again. Regardless of the reason, consider these sobering statistics:

FACTOID! According to the US Census Bureau, of the 2.5 million people who marry each year in the United States, more than 1.1 million are remarrying.

Median Age at second marriage:	Male: 34 Female: 32
Median Age at second divorce:	Male: 39.3 Female: 37
Median duration of first marriages which end in divorce:	Male: 7.8 years Female: 7.9 years
Median duration of second marriage that end in divorce:	Male: 7.3 years Female: 6.8 years
Number of years people wait to remarry:	Male: 3.3 years Female: 3.1 years
Percentage of remarried people who reach 5th, 10th, and 15th anniversary	5th: 82 percent 10th: 65 percent 15th: 42 percent

REMARRIAGE—ONLY THE BRAVE NEED APPLY
"I Will" is the shortest sentence in the English language . . .
"I Do" is the longest.

So, knowing all of this, should you forget about getting married again and instead open that intimate restaurant you've always dreamed about? That's probably not a good idea as restaurants are known to have the highest rate of failures of all businesses and they fail at an even higher rate that second marriages do. Before you hang up your apron for good, understand that a second marriage presents it own unique challenges. Though you think you may know more the second time around, you are in for a rude awakening as you cannot depend solely on your experience in choosing the next person to marry. Don't be fooled by the outside packaging for one minute. It may look, smell, taste, and feel the same, but there is often a lot more inside that is invisible to the human eye. Along with your new spouse comes a new set of in-laws, perhaps brother and sister-in-laws, and his or her friends who can't wait to critique you and hand your partner their evaluation cards.

Accordingly, before you say I do again, you must identify all that went wrong the first time around and then learn what to do to prevent those mistakes from happening again. You also have to be ready to say I do, again. A big part of getting ready is to understand what you have been through and what it will take to recover, rehabilitate, and move forward. With that information, you will be able to walk down the aisle and begin the journey of marital bliss.

PRACTICAL POINT: The divorce process makes one vulnerable and weak. No matter how bad things were, there is the human element of wanting to be with instead of being without. But if you were trolling for fish, you wouldn't keep the ones that were too small and should have been thrown back into the water. Similarly, when contemplating remarriage, you shouldn't settle for less either.

♛ REASONS FOR THE HIGH RATE OF FAILED REMARRIAGES
Why is the divorce rate for remarriages so high? Well studies show that people entering a second marriage sincerely believe that whatever went wrong the first time will not happen the second time around. They will blame their marriage downfall on being naïve, too young, inexperienced,

or just too overwhelmed with the idea of getting married that they did not pause long enough to figure out what it takes to stay married.

All that may sound good and support the rationale that no one is perfect and entitled to make a mistake. Researchers have concluded there may be specific reasons that lead to a remarriage downfall.

- *A remarriage has one of the same partners who was present in your last marriage*

  Most people don't take the time to evaluate WHAT went wrong. Instead, they just assume the problem was the WHO. Unfortunately that's not the case. It's important to look at what happened to cause the marriage to deteriorate. While it's tempting to assume that your Ex-spouse was the problem, they weren't 100 percent responsible. Without taking the time to look at YOUR part in the marriage's demise, you are destined to repeat history, if not make the same exact mistakes.

- *Divorced people often remarry quickly and find themselves living with a rebound or transitional person*

  Many times a person chooses remarriage strictly for emotional or security reasons. By remarrying too quickly, your new spouse only provided for your immediate needs and will soon become someone you do not want to spend a lifetime with.

- *A divorce experience doesn't suddenly reveal special awareness of relationship danger signs*

  Unfortunately, people jump into new relationships way too quickly after their divorce. They are not truly prepared to be in a committed relationship in the way that a new marriage requires. Most people are still reeling from the many changes and/or losses they experienced as a result of their divorce. But continuing to be wrapped up in what happened in your last marriage doesn't build a stable foundation for a new one.

- *Remarriage commitment is less than in a first marriage*

  Being in a remarriage situation means one member of your man and wife team has been married before. If the previous marriage ended in divorce this is an indication that a conscious decision was made to terminate the marriage. That's a boundary which was crossed over. After that boundary is breached once, it is much easier to come to that conclusion again. Divorce isn't an unknown entity. You may not have liked it but you endured it. Because of this, it becomes a more viable option than it did in a first marriage as soon as things start to get rough.

- *A step family is an unknown in our society*

  Step families are quickly becoming the most common family unit, but does anyone have a clue how they are supposed (to) work? We still base our ideas of family life on the old standard of a nuclear family (mom, dad, and their biological children). A step family does not fit this mold. When new step families see that their family doesn't come close to resembling what they expected, it's common for them to start questioning their decision to be together.

- *Children from a prior marriage places more stress on the newly formed union*

  While a couple is trying to build their new relationship, one or both spouses may also be attempting to balance the needs of their children. As a result, loyalties and interference from ex- spouses as well as present ones may strain the marriage to the breaking point.

- *There is no longer the stigma to divorce*

  Before the women's liberation movement came along, the word divorce was almost taboo. People often stayed married to each other for the sake of the children. That doesn't mean there still wasn't infidelity, verbal abuse, and more. With the passing of time, society as a whole shunned the notion of a couple splitting up. So what went on behind closed doors stayed shut to the outside world.

Sometime during the early 70's, when many states abandoned the requirement to show fault such as cruelty, abandonment, abuse, and infidelity and adopted a "no fault" requirement, a divorce revolution started in this country that has not ended. Divorce became easier to obtain and more common than not. By the 1990's the phrase "Single Mom" was part of our every day vernacular. The whole feeling about divorce has shifted from one of abhorrence to acceptable.

FACTOID: Celebrities have not been the best role models for the institution of marriage. Consider Elizabeth Taylor who has been married nine times, unless you count the ex-husband she remarried, Larry King has had six trips down the aisle. Billy Bob Thornton is one behind Larry. Tom Cruise's marriage to Katie was number three as was Jennifer Lopez's and she was not even thirty when she married the third time. The list of reckless celebrity marriages and divorces goes on and on. Even Prince Charles found something he didn't like about

Lady Di and wed Penelope (shouldn't this be (have been_) Camila Bowles instead?). Heavyweight contenders for the White House are not immune either as Rudy Giuliani has had his dirty sheets aired in public and so has Senator McCain.

- ***Younger couples reflect upon their first time around as a "starter marriage"***

    Many people in their twenties have what we now commonly call "starter marriages" wherein if they discover that they are not compatible, they divorce and marry someone else never looking back on the first relationship as nothing more than a first attempt at marriage. Likewise, the fact that things did not work out is not viewed as a failure but a learning experience for the next one or even the one after that. Lifetime Television produced a series starring Debra Messing called The Starter Wife which further validated this lifestyle.

THE STIGMA MAY BE GONE BUT WOMEN ARE STILL THE BIGGER LOSERS IN MULTIPLE MARRIAGES

It seems more stereotypes fall by the way side as we mature. The one that appears to be sticking around is how women who have had multiple marriages are viewed by society.

In the days of old Henry the VIII, his wives suffered the ultimate penalty of beheading when they divorced their husband. Today's modern woman does not face such a terrible fate but often their reputation does if they have had several marriages under their belt.

To illustrate, When Judy Nathan and Rudy Giuliani revealed six marriages between them, the former mayor of New York was not chastised by his political opponents though his wife took the media hit being labeled as a home wrecker. Going further back in political history, Adlai Stevenson's divorce probably cost him the election as president when he ran for the White House in 1952 and '56. But it wasn't much of a political problem for Republican presidential nominee Senator John McCain who had been married before.

❦ SO IS LIVING TOGETHER THE ANSWER?

Most of us would certainly never buy a car unseen. Even then, you would surely want to test drive it before you took out your checkbook. However, whether you and your Ex tested the goods and lived together before your first marriage does not necessarily mean you should live together with your fiancé or fianceé before you say I do, again.

❦ WHY COUPLES CHOOSE TO LIVE TOGETHER

Besides the obvious reason of being able to have sex 24/7, there are many other reasons why you may have lived with your Ex before your first marriage:

- Economical (it's cheaper to live as two than one)
- Practical (we see each other every day now anyway)
- Concern that if I do not commit, we may never tie the knot
- To do a trial run before marriage
- Tired of living with my family
- Escape from family home
- It's better than living alone
- A date has already been set to get married

Testing the equipment and making sure that everything works below the belt is certainly an important consideration before remarriage as discussed in Part Three. Although some of the reasons above may make perfect sense, living together may not always be the smart thing to do. In fact, according to the U.S, Census Bureau, more than fifty percent of couples who live together before remarriage end up apart either through just moving out or divorcing later on. Therefore, unless you heed the warning signs before you say I do, again, you will have two losses in the record book and your chances of getting drafted by another team will start to look bleak.

In addition, some studies also suggest that living together can be more stressful than being married and may result in a greater risk for divorce. The studies cite the following reasons:

- People who live together may be more accepting of divorce and are therefore less committed to marriage
- They may have married for the wrong reason, e.g., pressure from family, or having a child together
- They may think they know all there is to know about marriage already

- They may have too many high expectations of married life and get disillusioned early in their marriage
- They often have poor conflict resolution skills
- They may not be able to handle financial decisions together

LISA AND FRANK'S STORY

Lisa was forty-two, had a son named Dennis, who had just graduated high school. She had been divorced for over ten years. By the terms of her divorce, her Ex only had to pay child support until the child reached his eighteenth birthday. Dennis was enrolled in a community college, working full time, and found a friend to rent an apartment with.

With Dennis out of the home, Lisa thought it was time that she move on with her life. She began dating and soon met Frank. Frank was divorced and renting an apartment.

Within six months, and with marriage on their minds, they agreed it made more sense to live together as they were already spending almost all of their free time with each other. They also realized how much money they would save in rent only needing one apartment, especially since Lisa was no longer receiving child support.

However, within a few weeks of moving in together, Lisa noticed a change in Frank; he avoided conversations about setting a wedding date and told their friends that "society put too much emphasis on marriage." They did eventually get married but only after Lisa threatened to move out. However, the marriage lasted only one year.

Lisa's remarriage may have been doomed regardless of whether she moved in with Frank or not. However, his "why buy the cow when I get the milk for free" attitude illustrated his lack of commitment to marriage.

ৠ THE LEGALITIES OF LIVING TOGETHER BEFORE MARRIAGE

Along with the sobering statistics of failed remarriages for people who first live together, there are sometimes not so apparent legal reasons why living together may not be the best thing to do. Consider the following:

- ***You cannot make health care or financial decisions for each other***
  A power of attorney allows a non-relative to make financial and medical decisions for you if you are unexpectedly incapacitated. Un-

less you have each executed a power of attorney naming each other, you cannot make health care decisions for your significant other. To illustrate, if he gets sick and you find yourself in the emergency room, the doctor will still need to talk to a family member before any health care can be provided.

- ***You cannot file joint tax returns***
  There are tax benefits that are afforded to persons who are married that cannot be claimed if you are single.

- ***You cannot claim an automatic interest in assets acquired if it doesn't work out***
  If you are married and the marriage fails, depending on where you reside, you may have rights to the property even if your name is not on it. Only a handful of states recognize a non married partner's rights to property acquired while the two parties lived together but not married. Therefore, if you do not live in such a state, you would have to sue in a civil court arguing a partnership theory that gives you a right to claim an interest in the property.

WHAT THE NEXT DIVORCE MAY COST YOU!

Definition of divorce— the future tense of marriage.

When a marriage fails, losses are measured both emotionally as well as what remains in your pocketbook. However, despite being through one divorce, people are anxious to give marriage another try. Before you walk, jog, or race down the aisle, consider what the next divorce may cost you.

♛ CALCULATING THE EMOTIONAL ASSESSMENT EXPENSE

"I committed myself when I repeated the vows of devotion. How could he deceive me that way? I feel used and taken."
Or
"Life was perfect. Our wedding day was the happiest day of my life. I gave up something of mine that I can never get back!"

Do these phrases sound familiar? I have heard these words echoed hundreds of times from my clients as the emotional costs of divorce cannot be measured. Though friends and family members love to proclaim that "time is the greatest healer," when you are alone with your thoughts the memories of what went wrong often overshadow all the good times you had.

Accordingly, before booking a second trip down the aisle, take inventory of everything that went wrong the first time and all that you had to endure after you decided the marriage could not be saved. I refer to this exercise as your emotional assessment expense. While a specific dollar amount cannot be assigned to this expense, it did cost you part of your life. The next question you must ask is whether you are willing to incur this expense or more if the next marriage doesn't work out.

PRACTICAL POINT: In a fairy tale world, one does not need money when you have love. Love buys happiness as days are spent holding hands and staring profoundly into each other's eyes. There are no worries, no problems, and no sadness.

But then one day, one or both of you wake up and announce that you are no longer happy. You stop holding hands and stare at everyone else but one another. You are sad, angry, and cry. And (Also,) you blame yourself more than anyone else for allowing this to happen. The fairy tale does not have a happy ending.

♛ THE SOUNDS OF DIVORCE

"Marriage is a three ring circus: Engagement Ring, Wedding Ring, and suffering!"

The following is presented as a reminder of those days from the past you will want to avoid from reappearing in your future.

Whether you live in a state that requires proving grounds for divorce or a no fault one where all that is needed is a statement by one spouse that the marriage cannot survive, the legal system has never been concerned with the reasons that bring people to divorce court. As the court system is required to be indifferent and maintain objectivity, divorce courts have instead established labels for grounds for divorce. Providing your situation fits into one of the categories, your divorce will be routinely granted and before you even exit the rear of the courtroom you will hear the next case being called. Though emotions are left at the steps of the courthouse as you enter, they are picked up again on the way out.

Attorneys are required to be advocates for their clients so that they can understand the issues and apply the applicable law while always maintaining their professionalism. It is forbidden for us to become emotionally involved in the case, yet we must be sensitive to our client's needs and wants. The key to being a successful attorney is to be a good listener so that you can understand the dynamics that are evolving between the husband and wife.

For the past thirty years, I have listened to the sounds of divorce and it is not pleasant. If you were to visit a courtroom today, chances are you would not hear harps and violins. In all likelihood, you'd probably hear an out-of-control percussion section instead. Divorce has a tendency to turn people's lives upside down and make them feel helpless for the future.

Likewise, divorce clients are generally not the easiest to represent. Outside of the attorney's office or courtroom they may be kind, great parents, best friends, and loyal employees. But understandably, a person going through a divorce is experiencing a most emotionally trying time. In fact, research has shown that next to having a love one die, divorce ranks second as the most emotional time of your life. This includes the yelling, screaming, and finger pointing. Clients are short-tempered and they feel used, abused, cheated, and oftentimes need a sounding board. Most of the time, that sounding board is the attorney whom they use as an outlet to vent their anger.

Divorce brings out the worst in one's personality and often creates disruption for everyone under the radar screen who is associated with that person going through the divorce. And yes, time does heal the wounds but it never erases the memories.

🐚 THE HIGH COST OF DIVORCING

"Marriage is grand and divorce is about ten grand."

From a business point of view, marriage is a long-term investment. Accordingly, as you recite your vows, you are investing your future in the person you have agreed to marry. Consequently, as in any investment, you are looking to earn a return on your investment which is often measured by the pleasures you receive from being married.

PRACTICAL POINT! If you were investing in a mutual fund, your broker is obligated to provide you with what is known as a risk analysis. That is, he would give you a history of how the fund has performed in the past. Based on this information, you would then decide if you want to invest with the understanding that you could lose money. Continuing this analysis, if a marriage fails, you have lost your investment. And though no investment is "risk free," in the world of divorce, second marriages are riskier investments. The time that you were together can prove to be very expensive when all is sorted through in divorce court. Therefore, it is prudent to proceed into marriage cautiously and evaluate the investment before you say I do, again.

☙ ATTORNEY FEES

If your first divorce was uncontested, meaning there were few if any issues to be resolved, you may have prepared the legal papers yourself or had a divorce service assist you. Even if you did retain an attorney, it is quite probable that you paid a flat fee based on the simplicity of the case.

However, most second marriage divorces include unresolved issues concerning child support, custody, and visitation as well as the division of property and debts. As a result, and because the attorney does not know whether the other spouse will be cooperative or hire an attorney who is out to make this the bloodiest and ugliest divorce proceeding of all-time, your attorney will take your case based on an hourly rate.

In addition, he will most likely ask you for a retainer fee which his time is billed against. To illustrate, if his hourly rate is $300 per hour, and he requires an upfront retainer fee of $3,000, you will not be billed for any additional time until he has performed 10 hours of work. I assure you that ten hours of legal time is used up rather quickly especially when there are issues of concerning custody, visitation, and support.

PRACTICAL POINT! An attorney bills for all his time related to your case. This may include speaking with you by phone, reading e-mail you sent him, having a conversation with your spouse's attorney, as well as the time it takes him to drive to and from court for your case.

PRACTICAL POINT: An attorney's hourly rate does vary from state to state. However, according to the 2007 Survey of Law Firm Economics, the average hourly rate is $279.

☙ ASSESSING HOW MUCH TO CHARGE

When a client first contacts our office seeking legal services, we try to assess by phone and prior to the initial face-to-face consultation what are the issues that need to be resolved. Specifically, we ask:

- Are you seeking spousal support? (alimony)
- Are you seeking child support?
- Are their issues regarding custody and visitation?
- Does a house have to be sold?
- What property needs to be divided?
  Is there a pension, 401K, or other retirement plan?
  Is there a business that has to be valued?
  Are there income taxes that are owed or tax issues to be resolved?
- Have you reached an agreement as to who will pay what bills?

In response, a client often tells us the following:

"I have everything worked out with my spouse and there are no issues. We just need to get the paperwork done."

In theory this may sound right but only a small percentage of second marriage divorces are that simple as "getting the paperwork done." In those rare cases where there are no issues to be resolved, an attorney may be willing to charge a flat fee to complete the work. This is known as an uncontested divorce. However, most attorneys, to protect themselves from issues that arise and were not disclosed to them by the client, will have the client sign an agreement acknowledging that the fee quoted will increase if additional work is required.

LEGALLY SPEAKING! Some states recognize what is commonly called "summary dissolutions." In these cases, many of the steps that apply in more complicated divorces are not required and the process moves along more quickly. To qualify, typically the length of marriage must not have exceeded three years, there are no children, and there is no real estate to be divided. www.findlaw.com is a great reference site that provides state by state law.

♔ OTHER RELATED COSTS

Representing a client in a divorce is labor intensive. That is, in addition to the attorney's time, he is using many resources to process your case. Accordingly, in addition to his time and the costs of filing, you may also be liable for the following:

- Postage
- Photocopying fees
- Telephone charges for faxing documents
- Messenger fees and other transportation charges

Furthermore, depending on the complexity of issues, the following may also apply:

- Fees to an accountant to evaluate a business
- Appraisal fees to determine real estate values
- Forensic costs to find assets that you believe your spouse has hidden
- Expert opinion fees for doctors to provide evaluation for issues concerning custody of children

♛ COSTS THAT CAN'T BE ASSESSED

Your time

Though your time certainly has value, it is not a cost that the court will recognize and reimburse you for. The time you had to spend in court seeking a divorce is lost forever.

The cost to your family and loved ones

As that highly popular commercial goes, there are certain things in life that are priceless. Certainly that includes the emotional cost to your family and friends as there is no conceivable way of measuring the toll a divorce takes on your loved ones.

♛ A MARRIAGE IS A BINDING AND LEGAL CONTRACT

The vows that are exchanged during the wedding ceremony represent the marriage contract. "To love . . ." are the promises recited between a husband and wife that they will honor the terms of the contract.

Compared to more complex contracts like an auto lease or an agreement to rent an apartment, the words that make up the marriage vows are very specific and generally not subject to interpretation. Therefore, "to love, honor, and cherish" does not mean to love until you are bored with your spouse or to cherish until someone better comes along.

Likewise, if one of the parties to the marriage contract breaches the vows, the contract may be dissolved. However, unlike other breach of contract actions where the remedy for the winning party is an award of

money, divorce courts are often required to divide property, assign responsibility for debts, order payment for child and spousal support, and make
decisions regarding custody and visitation. In addition, because issues of
support and custody are viewed as "in the best interest of the party," these
issues remain open and either party may later come into court to have the
problem reviewed or modified.

LEGALLY SPEAKING! Most states view a marriage of ten years or
more as a long-term marriage. As a result, unless the parties agree otherwise, the issue of spousal support or alimony remains open indefi-
nitely or unless the spouse who is awarded support dies or remarries.

THE LEGAL AND NONLEGAL CONSEQUENCES OF DIVORCE

"Instead of ever getting married again, I am going to find a woman I don't like and give her a house!"

Though the ink may have long dried on your court papers terminating your first marriage, the following is a reminder of some of the obvious and not so obvious legal consequences of your divorce.

⚜ TAX CONSEQUENCES

As alimony is the amount paid to a spouse for his or her living expenses, the person receiving the support must pay taxes on the alimony received in the year it is given. Likewise, the person paying the support may deduct the amount in the year it is paid. To deduct alimony, certain requirements must be made:

> LEGALLY SPEAKING! Child support is not taxable to the receiving spouse, nor can it be deducted by the paying spouse as the purpose of child support is to provide for the welfare of a child and therefore is not viewed as income.

❦ MARITAL STATUS

On all applications that ask what is your marital status, you must list it as divorced, not single. If, however, your marriage was annulled, you could legally state your status as "single" as the law views annulments as if you were never married.

❦ COURT ORDERS

As parents, we raise our children to behave properly. If they misbehave, there are consequences. Of course, the child's age will dictate what will be the nature of the penalty for their misbehavior.

Likewise, in a divorce, if a court makes an order and that order is not followed, the consequence for the violation may be a contempt of court action. The penalty could be as severe as imprisonment.

BETH'S STORY

Beth repeatedly refused to allow her ex husband regular visitation with their son. Though the court order provided for weekend visitation every week, she always came up with some reason to not permit visitation. Finally, after several hearings threatening her with contempt, the court stood by its threat and placed my client in custody for seventy-two hours. She went kicking and screaming to jail cursing the judge and me. Needless to say, I lost a client. However, she was wrong in not respecting a court order and ended up having to suffer the consequences.

❦ WHAT'S IN A NAME

When a husband and wife marry, the wife typically assumes her husband's last name. Unless the marriage license states a different last name for the wife, this becomes her legal last name and is to be used for reporting income to the IRS, for voting, for issuance of a driver's license, obtaining a passport and other governmental processes that require that you state your legal name.

Upon petitioning for divorce, the wife may request that the Court restore her former name. Accordingly, her last name will be changed legally upon the finalization of the divorce. If, however, she decides not to make such a request, but later wants to legally change her name, she would have to file for a formal name change. This is a separate court proceeding that requires additional filing fees and court costs as well as a court appearance.

LEGALLY SPEAKING! When there are young children of the marriage, often a spouse will elect not to change her name so as to avoid confusion with school records as well as other social issues concerning the children.

❦ ADOPTIONS ARE FOREVER

When a stepparent adopts a child from his spouse's previous relationship, the adoption survives any subsequent divorce action. That is, though the parents are terminating their relationship, the adopting parent is still legally responsible for the adopted child. By law, both parents are legally responsible for the care and welfare of their children. Furthermore, if child support is ordered to be paid by one spouse that will include payment of support for the adopted child. In addition, an adopted child has the same rights of inheritance and may be a recipient of social security benefits (if under age eighteen) as if he was a natural child of the marriage.

❦ GRANDPARENT RIGHTS

One of the most unfortunate consequences of divorce affects grandparents. This is because; divorce courts are terminating a marriage between a husband and wife. But the grandparents of the couple divorcing are not a part of the divorce proceeding. As a result, where there are children involved, many states have no provisions for grandparents to see their grandchildren as visitation rights are only extended to the non-custodial parent.

LEGALLY SPEAKING! Every year we receive dozens of calls from grandparents wanting to see their grandchildren. The parents have divorced and now, the parent who has custody is refusing visitation. Usually, there had not been a good relationship established between the mother and her in-laws during the marriage and she now feels no obligation to be nice to them. In California, like many states, unless grandparent rights are spelled out in the custody and visitation agreement, grandparents' rights are not automatic. Therefore, often grandparents have to retain an attorney to file a petition seeking visitation.

❦ DON'T COUNT ON THAT INHERITANCE

Property that is acquired through an inheritance belongs to the spouse that the property is left to as stated in a trust or will. In some states, like California, if the acquiring spouse subsequently transfers that property into the names of both spouses, it then becomes the property of both the husband and wife. Likewise, as a result of a divorce, any future expectations of receiving an interest in an inheritance would be terminated as a result of the divorce.

❦ RECIPROCAL POWERS OF ATTORNEY THAT NAME BOTH HUSBAND AND WIFE ARE NOT ENFORCEABLE

If you and your spouse are both named as having powers of attorney for another, the effect of a divorce terminates that appointment. That is because the person making the appointment chose both you and your spouse. Legally, your legal relationship with your spouse has terminated and therefore the language of the power of attorney cannot be enforced.

❦ THE I.R.S. AND UNCLE SAM STILL WANTS YOU!

Up until the most recent overhaul of the tax codes, the Internal Revenue Service has favored married couples over single persons granting a husband and wife a more favorable tax bracket when filing tax returns. While the inequity between persons filing single and married couples has been somewhat corrected, married couples still fare better than single filers regarding how much Uncle Sam wants.

For this reason, many divorcing couples are advised by their tax preparer to still file a joint return, even if their divorce has been finalized. Of course, for the following taxable year, that benefit would no longer apply and each spouse would be required to report any income as a single person.

❦ INSURANCE AND DIVORCE

Statistically, persons who divorce and do not marry again die sooner than married couples. Also, divorced persons have a higher incident of health problems than married folks. For these reasons, both health and life insurance providers rate single persons higher than those married, resulting in single people having to paying (pay) higher insurance premiums.

✿ MUST MAKE IT TO TEN YEARS FOR SOCIAL SECURITY BENEFITS

A person is eligible to receive social security retirement benefits as early as age sixty-two, though most persons choose to wait and apply when they are sixty-five.

However, if you are married for less than ten years, you are not entitled to a portion of your spouse's social security benefits when he retires or becomes disabled.

✿ THE FINANCIAL FALLOUT FROM A DIVORCE

Though the Court has signed the final decree terminating the marriage, the financial ramifications of divorce may be felt for years to come. This is especially true when there are children as issues concerning custody, visitation, and support may always be revisited by the Court upon the petition of either spouse. And though financially both men and women suffer after a divorce, a 2002 U.S. Census Bureau statistic showed that a woman's standard of living plummeted more than 73 percent the first year following her divorce.

✿ THE TRAVEL PENALTIES FOR BEING SINGLE

If you have ever looked into booking a cruise, check the small print which explains the surcharge you must pay for wanting to take that trip. Fares are based on two persons sharing the same cabin. So if you are traveling alone and do not want to be paired up with a stranger, you will pay an additional 50 percent.

✿ HEALTH INSURANCE BENEFITS ARE TERMINATED UPON DIVORCE

A spouse who is ordered to pay child support usually must also provide health insurance for children of the marriage. However, such an order rarely is extended to the other spouse. As a result, that spouse must now secure his or her own insurance which can be very expensive, especially if she has any preexisting conditions.

✿ THAT'S WHAT FRIENDS WERE FOR

In addition to the division of both real estate and personal property, friends of the divorced couple often decide whom they will continue to have a social relationship with and which spouse will be kicked to the curb.

JANICE'S STORY

My friend Janice and I met in college. We were single but were dating other people and were in serious relationships. We both married and soon thereafter my wife and I moved to California. When an employment opportunity arose for Janice, she and her husband also moved west where we picked up our friendship again. Unfortunately, Janice and Carl had marital problems and divorced. However, Carl has often reminded me of his wife's parting words: "To be fair, I'll take the piano and you get Ben and Phyllis!"

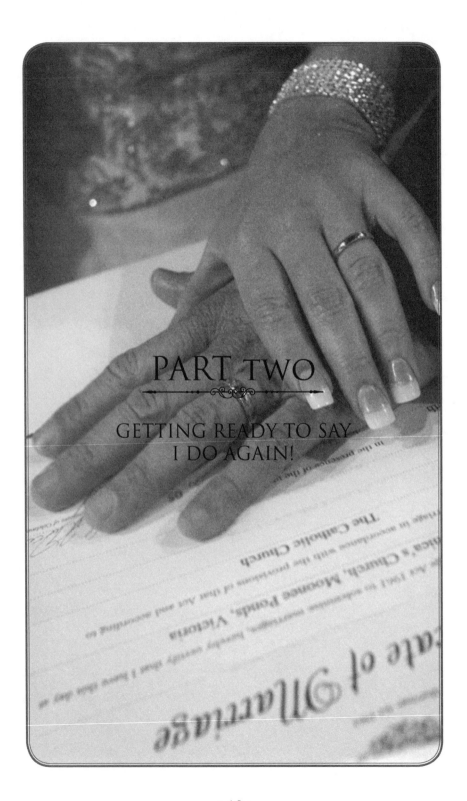

PART TWO

GETTING READY TO SAY
I DO AGAIN!

GETTING EMOTIONALLY READY TO SAY I DO AGAIN!

If your first marriage was reported as a news event, it might sound something likes this:

> *"Cindy Clark's two year marriage to Josh Clark ended in divorce today when a Superior Court ruled there were irreconcilable differences that lead to the irremediable breakdown of the marriage. Both parties were unavailable for comment."*

Though this sounds cold, indifferent, and unemotional, every day hundreds of marriages are dissolved by the stroke of a pen. What often remains, however, are fractured lives and whopping legal bills.

As hard as it may seem to believe, there is definitely a life after divorce that can be even more exciting, vibrant, and fulfilling than the first marriage. To get there, you must first separate yourself from any emotional issues that tie you to your first marriage. Until that time, the invitations, the cake, and yes, your fiancé must be put on hold.

♛ EMOTIONALLY ENDING YOUR FIRST MARRIAGE

Q: "What should you do if you see your ex spouse rolling around in pain on the ground?"
A: "Shoot him again!"

Just because you can hold a piece of paper that says you are divorced may not necessarily mean you have emotionally accepted that your marriage has ended. This is especially true where only one spouse wanted the divorce. Until you are no longer spending your days grieving about your marriage, you are not ready to say I do, again.

PRACTICAL POINT: The court process has restored your status as a single person and (if female) you may have requested that your maiden name also be returned. However, that piece of paper will have no meaning to you until you emotionally accept you are single again. Only then can you move on with your life and consider sharing it with someone new.

REBECCA'S STORY

Rebecca was blindsided when her husband announced he wanted a divorce. She thought she had the fairy tale marriage; house, two beautiful kids, and an adoring husband. As it turned out, however, he was adoring someone else. Even after her divorce was final, Rebecca said she continued to wear her wedding band for the next year as she could not accept that the marriage was really over.

♛ WHY THE FIRST MARRIAGE FAILED?

Emotional preparation for saying I do again requires an understanding of why your first marriage ended.

In preparing material for this book, I asked clients to write down the qualities they admired most about the person they planned to marry and to pick the one particular quality that made them want to walk down the aisle. I then asked my clients to list the main reason for their divorce. The answers may surprise you as there were often only subtle differences between the initial attraction and the distraction, though it was significant enough to end the marriage.

CHAPTER FOUR

Of course, being a "Monday morning quarterback" is priceless. But, before you rush to say I do, again, analyze the reasons why you are no longer with your former spouse to prevent making the same mistake twice.

REASONS FOR DIVORCE

- I married my husband because he could protect me.
  I divorced him because he was too dominating.

- I married her because I fell in love with this fragile and petite person.
  I divorced her because she was weak and helpless.

- I married my husband because I knew he would be able to provide for us and that gave me a sense of security.
  I divorced him because he was married to his work.

- I married her because she had the same qualities of my mother whom I so admire.
  I divorced her because she way too motherly and less of a wife.

- I married him because he was a free spirit.
  I divorced him because he had no goals or ambition.

- I married him because he was responsible and organized.
  I divorced him because he was so rigid and not spontaneous enough.

- I married him because he had this great personality that everyone loved.
  I divorced him because he would not stop the flirting.

- I married him because he was so responsible with money.
  I divorced him because he was so cheap.

- I married him because he was in such great physical shape.
  I divorced him because his number one priority was working out.

- I married him because he was so protective which made me feel safe.
  I divorced him because I felt trapped.

- I married him because he sexually satisfied me more than any other man.
  I divorced him because he was a sexual addict.

- I married him because he loved to travel.
  I divorced him because he did not know how to sit still.

- I married her because she smothered me with attention.
  I divorced her because she was too possessive and did not let me breathe.

PRACTICAL POINT: Are you feeling guilty about your divorce? Do you blame yourself? In retrospect, would you do things differently now if given the chance? The best way to deal with any guilt you are having is to enroll in a support group where you can meet other people who share your feelings and concerns. Support groups are typically free or have a nominal charge. Start by contacting the city where you reside. You can also search the Internet for referrals in your community.

✿ ESTABLISHING A NEW CIRCLE OF FRIENDS

As a married couple, there are your friends that you had before marriage, your spouse's friends, and then there are your mutual friends. However, often, in a divorce, friends take sides as they charge and convict whom they believe is the culpable party without you having the benefit of a trial. Accordingly, take inventory to determine who your true friends are and which ones are friends in name only.

✿ QUESTIONS TO ASK YOURSELF ABOUT YOUR FRIENDS:

Do your friends support that you are single again?
Do your friends solely blame you for the divorce?
Do your friends make you feel uncomfortable by always making references to your Ex?

♛ GETTING RID OF BAGGAGE

"I must admit you brought religion into my life. I never believed in hell until I divorced you!"

When a marriage fails, the material things are often divided between the spouses. But you cannot divide emotion. The memories of both the good and bad times will stay with you for a long time. But in getting emotionally ready to remarry, you need to rid yourself of the emotional baggage you are still carrying and that is weighing you down. You cannot enter into a new relationship until you have cast off all those negative feelings. If you do not, you will most likely drag this baggage into your next relationship. As a result, though you are trying to stay afloat, your baggage will always pull you under. Here are some things you can do.

♛ ESTABLISH A NEW YOU

Q. Why are married women heavier than single women?
A. Single women come home, see what's in the fridge and go to bed. Married women come home, see what's in bed, and then go to the fridge.

Have you seen the ABC show ***Extreme Makeover***—Home Edition? The basic premise is that a truly deserving family has their home remodeled. Everyone is so excited as the camera takes the viewer from room to room showing the before and after.

After a divorce, clients often tell us that they need to feel better about themselves. Perhaps it is doing something as simple as getting a new hair style, joining a gym, or trading in that gas guzzling SUV for a sleek new coupe. And with the continued acceptance of cosmetic surgery, facelifts, tummy tucks, and more, these are no longer just for the pleasures of the rich and famous.

You don't have to take such drastic measures to have a new and improved you. It can include joining a singles group, taking on a new hobby, or deciding that you need new friends in your life who share your interests. The Internet is an inexpensive way to explore common interests as joining groups. For example, on the home page of Yahoo, there is a link to

"Groups." Simply by typing in your interests, you will be amazed at what is available. The bottom line is that it is your life and you need to discover what you feel passionate about.

TODAY'S 50 MAY NOT ALWAYS BE YESTERDAY'S 40

Oprah, Ellen, and numerous other talk shows, as well as magazines, have been touting that today's fifty-year-old is yesterday's forty. The point is people who are older now are more active than their parents were when they were the same age. This is probably correct as the baby boomer generation is more in tuned with eating right, exercising, and taking better care of your self. If you feel good, it is only logical that you will take the time to look better.

Of course, no one will object to wanting to look better. What causes concerns, however, are those persons who are in search of the fountain of youth and are trying to recapture the way they looked years ago.

But remember, though you have moved past the divorce, resolved all of the emotional issues, and are both legally and financially in shape to consider saying I do, again, the one thing you cannot do is turn back the clock to the time before you said I do the first time!

☗ ACCEPTING WHAT YOU LOOK LIKE

Looking in your closet, the jeans you wore ten years ago may not fit the same anymore. You may even be a few or a lot more pounds heavier, your body may have taken on a new shape, and gravity is causing the parts of your anatomy that used to point up droop down toward your toes. Physical changes over time should not set off an alarm to run to the closest plastic surgeon and beg for a head to toe make over.

LONNIE'S STORY

In Lonnie's divorce, the court ordered that her Ex pay her child support. A year later, she was back in our office because her husband had fallen seriously behind in his payments and she wanted to pursue a contempt of court action against him.

As is my custom, I greet each client in the reception room and walk them back to my office. Now I will admit that I am terrible at remembering faces but Lonnie's was so drastically changed from the last time I had seen her. She was almost impossible to recognize. In my office, Lonnie admitted that she had used a large portion of her divorce settlement money on plastic surgery as she thought she needed a drastic change to improve her chances of ever remarrying. Unfortunately, from my point of view, it was not money well spent as the end result was anything but attractive.

♕ ESTABLISHING YOUR INDEPENDENCE

In the twenty-first century, modern thinking husbands and wives, often throw out the window when asked about any stereotypes in the marriage. The only word bantered about is equality. Well this makes for a good discussion on talk radio, but in the real world there are still stereotypes in marriage and they are not all bad. For example, there is nothing wrong in admitting that the husband takes out and brings in the garbage cans and the wife does the grocery shopping and picks up the clothes at the dry cleaners.

When a couple divorces, the roles that you depended on your spouse to do now rests solely upon your shoulders. As a result, you have more responsibilities and being emotionally ready to say I do again requires that you accept these roles and not rush to find someone else to do them for you.

PRACTICAL POINT! The number one reason given why people remarry too soon is that they were too use to having someone do things for them. You must accept the fact that groceries will not magically appear in your refrigerator, that wrinkle-free pants still have to be hung up, and the cable will be shut off unless you write a check. Being single again means taking responsibility for yourself.

♕ TAKING INVENTORY OF YOURSELF BEFORE YOU SAY I DO, AGAIN

In my thirty plus years of practice, I think I have probably heard every reason for why a marriage failed. One client even told me that "his marriage was doomed from the moment he said I do." I did want to ask him if he at least enjoyed the honeymoon but retained my professionalism and I kept my mouth shut instead.

Accordingly, if the person standing beside you at the altar was anything but the individual you thought you were marrying, it should not have been a surprise that your marriage did not work out. But, to improve your chances, part of getting ready to say I do again includes taking inventory of yourself and recognizing anything you may need to change before you tie the knot again. The following are a few questions to ponder in evaluating your first marriage:

- Were you too aggressive when you should have been more passive?
- Were you too self-absorbed when you should have been more caring?
- Were you too opinionated when you should have been listening attentively?
- What did you do that worked so well?
- What always failed?
- Did you try to make it work or sit on the sidelines and watch it fail?

TOP TEN MARRIAGE FLAWS

It is easy to blame the other person and difficult to admit fault. When polled, the following examples were most often cited by our clients for what they felt they were guilty of. Upon review, all of us at one time or another has committing (have committed) these acts. In evaluating your first marriage, review this list to determine if any of these apply to you.

1. Not listening to your spouse
2. Not showing respect
3. Insisting that you were always right
4. Being dishonest, selfish, or self-centered
5. Being self-absorbed with only what benefits you
6. Making fun of and ridiculing your spouse in front of family and friends
7. Lack of sexual interest
8. Not being truthful
9. Being annoying, moody, obnoxious, or having a temper
10. Just not fun to be around

♛ ACCEPT BEING SINGLE AGAIN!

At the end of my car lease, my wife always comments that I have no emotional attachment to the car that I drive as I view it as renting someone's property. This philosophy, however, should not apply to a marriage as it is very difficult to transit from one marriage to another.

During this transition period, you must first learn to accept your new status as a single person before you can emotionally say I do again. Accordingly, if any of the following behavior applies to you, it is now time to change.

- I shy away from invitations as I know I will be the only single person there.
- I know my married friends have excluded me from social gatherings that involve husbands and wives.

- I hate the look I get when I ask for "One movie ticket, please."
- Going to a singles mixer is like being put in a cage. I feel I am on display for all to see.
- I feel like a marked person with a sign on my head that says "loser".
- When I tell someone I am single, I feel I am negatively judged.
- Sometimes I put on my wedding band just to avoid the weirdoes from approaching me.

♛ GETTING YOUR CHILDREN EMOTIONALLY READY FOR YOU TO SAY I DO AGAIN

If you have children, remarriage is a big change for those who have already experienced a great deal of change they didn't ask for. Though your kids may be content with your dating, once an engagement is announced, it makes the upcoming changes more real to them. That's when resistance can set in.

The most common reason for this behavior occurs when the child has seen his parent already hurt from the other parent. They simply do not want Mom to get hurt again and will view the step-parent as the enemy.

WAYNE'S STORY

Wendy had two daughters from her first marriage. She waited two years after her divorce before she started dating again. Wendy met Wayne who had never been married before. When she told the girls that she was seeing someone, the oldest said that she didn't want to have "two daddies." When the girls met Wayne, he was given the cold shoulder. Despite the first meeting, they continued to date. When Wayne suggested that the four of them go camping for the weekend, it was as if he was watching his own version of the movie Parent Trap as the girls did everything imaginable to sabotage his relationship with their mother.

For a more complete discussion of remarriage and blended families, please see Chapter Twenty-three.

♛ EMOTIONALLY PREPARING OTHERS BEFORE YOU SAY I DO AGAIN!

It's not just your children you have to worry about too before you say I do, again. What about your own immediate family? This remarriage thing may be new to them and they aren't sure what the proper etiquette is. How will holidays be spent now? Are they responsible for gifts to step-grandchildren they hardly know? Another thing to consider (,) is they may have loyalty conflicts with your previous spouse. They may fear you getting hurt again because they may have helped you pick up the pieces from the previous loss.

These same concerns may be present with your friends. Whereas with a first engagement, friends offer a sincere and heart-felt, "Congratulations." You may get a, "Are you sure about this?" this time around. Again, this is probably born out of a concern for you not getting hurt.(but) But it can still make you feel as if your bubble has just been bursted.(burst)

Was Wanting Him to Change Really All About You?

Men marry women with the hope they will never change. Women marry men with the hope they will change. Invariably they are both disappointed. —Albert Einstein

PRACTICAL POINT: The majority of the material found in this book is of equal interest to both sexes. However, this section is especially applicable to women.

D id your first marriage fail because you spent your married life trying to change your Ex? In retrospect, were your expectations too unrealistic? In the end, were the changes you wanted really that important?

☙ HE'S JUST NOT WIRED THAT WAY!

Whether you are divorced once, twice, or more, and have had countless short or long-term relationships, regardless of your age you firmly, adamantly, and unequivocally believe that you can change him. This also applies if you have only met him casually, spoken to him on the phone, or perhaps you've actually never met him.

The truth, ladies, however, is that it just ain't so. Why? Simply put, guys are not wired that way. To illustrate, my wife has complained for more than thirty years of marriage that I do not get a close enough shave when I shave in the shower. Guess what? I still shave in the shower. I don't take the time to think about getting out of the shower to shave just so that I get a closer shave. All I am thinking about is that I need to shave.

Likewise, women are also more detailed oriented and often complain to their partner that they do not take notice of things, big or small. For instance, I can't remember what I wore yesterday even if my life depended on it. My wife on the other hand can recall what she or I wore at someone's party a year ago. When a woman meets someone for the first time, she sizes that person from head to toe. It is as if you are passing through an X-ray scanner at the airport and every article of clothing and body characteristic is being analyzed including:

- The type of shoes you are wearing
- Your choice and style of clothes
- Are your clothes ironed
- The color and style of your hair
- Whether your teeth are white and straight
- Your posture
- Your hands (and if female your choice of nail polish)
- Do you have a nice smile
- The color of your eyes

UNDERSTANDING THE ELECTRICAL BLUEPRINT OF MEN AND WOMEN

Most women believe men have only one wire that goes from their brain to what is hanging between their legs. As a guy, I can tell you with certainty that they are dead wrong. There is a also a wire that goes from our brain to our stomachs, another that controls the TV remote, one that helps us hear you and understood though this particular wire is often broken, and finally there are a few others that help us make simple decisions but do not allow multi-tasking. In comparison, women have this vast network of wires that travel around from their head to their toes, and goes around, transverse, do figure eights, cross over, lasso, and then send different messages at the same time which are often difficult to understand, causing mass confusion to men but are completely understood by women.

Despite having this awareness, women still enter into marriage believing they can perform surgery and transform their spouse into someone he was not before, only to realize that after trial and error, not to mention a river of tears, they did not succeed. Then they go on to enter a second marriage carrying the same misbelief.

In reality, you may enjoy changing your hairstyle every few years and need that new handbag when spring becomes summer. However getting a man to change his blue shirt with palm trees because it has a stain on it, put the plate and glass in the sink (but not in the dishwasher) after he has eaten the dinner you left for him, or order Salmon instead of his 24 ounce steak is pushing the limit. If you sincerely believe otherwise that through by using your magical feminine wiles you can still change him, I want to sell you some swamp land in Florida! Accordingly, as you contemplate a second marriage, the only thing that is pretty predictable he will change is his underwear and even that is no guarantee!

THINGS THAT DO NOT COME NATURALLY FOR MOST MEN?

Most men:
- Are not into family gatherings, his or yours
- Do not make a big deal about celebrating holidays
- Do not go window shopping and only buys what he needs
- Do not enjoy going shopping with you for you
- Cannot wrap presents to save his life
- Cannot set a table for company
- Do not understand the attraction to Oprah
- Do not like "chick" flicks
- Are not into museums of art
- Do not put the toilet seat up
- Don't ask for directions
- Do not write thank you notes
- Do not hear you when watching TV
- Do not remember what you wore yesterday
- Do not offer compliments unless there is something in it for them
- Do not massage your feet unless there is something in it for them
- Do not give back rubs unless there is something in it for them
- Do not call at least once during the day just to check in
- Do not routinely ask how is your mother or sister

- Do not wipe the glass door after showering
- Have a different definition of what it means to be nice, friendly, and kind
- Do not put the dirty dishes in the sink
- Do not load or unload the dishwasher
- Do not do laundry unless they have no clean clothes left
- Do not enjoy shopping (this one needs to be repeated)
- Do not send flowers unless they did something very bad
- Do not care to hear about your girlfriends unless she is hot and single
- Do not know what is a "duvet" and don't care to know
- Do not read the greeting card you gave him word for word
- Do not read the greeting card he is purchasing for you word for word
- Do not add extensive personal notes on greeting cards he is sending
- Will not suggest going to a "chick flick"
- Do not make impulse purchases
- Do not pick up their dirty socks and put them in the laundry basket
- Do not buy something fun instead of always buying what is practical
- Will not actually look forward to going to a couples baby shower
- Cannot make the bed as good as you can
- Are not warm and fuzzy and more
- Do not understand your emotional needs
- Are not comfortable with your acts of public affection
- Are not comfortable holding your purse in public
- Don't understand menopause
- Are fashionably early and don't understand that you will be there at "10 ish"
- Do not understand fashion for you or him
- Apply logic before emotion
- Analyze before they emotionalize
- Are not good historians
- Describe things using only primary colors
- Are not descriptive in providing details
- Do not enjoy foreplay unless it is for him
- Describe sex as a physical act
- Describe making love as a physical act
- Do not want your help for home improvements
- Have a different definition than yours for love, emotion, happiness, and kindness
- Don't hear you when watching TV
- Would get into bed after exercising without showering first

YOU DON'T SEND ME FLOWERS ANYMORE

For those who remember the beautiful Neil Diamond ballad You Don't Send Me Flowers Anymore, Barbra Streisand laments there once was a time when she would receive unexpected flowers from her lover but that has now stopped. This is not to say there are not guys out there who send flowers without an occasion or offer to massage your back after you've had an extremely hard day. But if the Super Bowl or some other major sporting event is on the television, don't expect your guy to jump in the car to go with you to the mall. It is not that he doesn't. The trouble is he just does not think about things the way you do. Those rare times when he does consider it, it has no value or importance. So, when reviewing the above list, if your Ex was guilty of any of these, do not assume your next husband will be any different. Chances are, he will most likely not think the way you do. If this is that important to you, you should rethink remarriage altogether. Otherwise, accept the fact that it's not his fault. He's just not wired that way.

♛ WHAT BUGS MEN THE MOST ABOUT WOMEN

According to **Psychology Today** ,the following are what bugs men the most about their partners. You may be surprised that not wanting to have sex with your partner is not on the list:

#10   Your complaints about his choice and style of clothing
9   How often he wears the same clothes
8   What he orders in a restaurant
7   His choice of movies
6   Who his friends are
5   What he considers to be "fun"
4   What you perceive as his bad habits
3   Repeatedly asking "Is something bothering you?"
2   That he does not hear you
1   And the thing that bugs men most about women is her recalling of some event or something he said and making it an issue today!

Accordingly, scrutinizing yourself includes identifying what you may have done during your marriage that "bugged" your Ex. Consider the following:

MY FRIEND'S STORY

My wife and I were out to dinner with our friends. When the waiter asked for our orders, my friend said that he wanted the Halibut topped with capers in a cream sauce. His wife immediately responded that he should order something else as he surely wouldn't like it. They exchanged some words but he held his ground and ordered the Halibut. When his entree arrived, he said it was delicious. But throughout the dinner, she kept commenting that his food looked terrible. When he offered her a taste, she flat out refused.

This example may sound so trivial but have you ever suggested what he should order? Why on earth would you do that? Aside from dietary concerns which is a whole different discussion, at the end of the day, what is the big difference between him having the Halibut instead of the Salmon that you were sure he would like better?

♛ LOST IN TRANSLATION

"There are two times when a man doesn't understand a woman; before marriage and after marriage."

Even within the happiest of marriages, oftentimes one spouse complains that the other is not listening. To illustrate, my wife may ask me (most of the time she tells me point-blank) to do something. But when I return empty handed, she stares at me wondering, how do I manage to put my pants on every morning.

It is not that men don't listen; it is instead how we interpret what you are saying. Before you assume that your first marriage may have failed for lack of communication, consider the following story which was contributed to me by a friend.

THE DIFFERENCE BETWEEN MEN AND WOMEN

Let's say a guy named Roger is attracted to a woman named Elaine. He asks her out to dinner; she accepts; they have a pretty good time. A few nights later he asks her out again; and again they enjoy themselves. They continue to see each other regularly, and after a while neither one of them is seeing anybody else.

And then, one evening when they're driving home, a thought occurs to

Elaine, and, without really thinking, she says it aloud. "Do you realize that, as of tonight, we've been seeing each other for exactly six months?"
Then there is dead silence in the car.

To Elaine, it seems like a very loud and uncomfortable silence. She thinks to herself, *I wonder if it bothers him that I said that. Maybe he's been feeling confined by our relationship; maybe he thinks I'm trying to push him into some kind of obligation that he doesn't want, or isn't sure of.*

Roger is thinking, *Wow! Six months.*

And Elaine is thinking, *But, hey, I'm not so sure I want this kind of relationship, either. Sometimes I wish I had a little more space, so I'd have time to think about whether I really want us to keep going the way we are, moving steadily toward... I mean, where are we going? Are we just going to keep seeing each other at this level of intimacy? Are we heading toward marriage? Toward children? Toward a lifetime together? Am I ready for that level of commitment? Do I really even know this person?*

Roger is also thinking, *So, that means it was... let's see... February when we started going out, which was right after I had the car at the dealer's, which means...let me check the odometer... Whoa! I am way overdue for an oil change here.*

Meanwhile Elaine is thinking, *He's upset. I can see it on his face. Maybe I'm reading this completely wrong.* Maybe he wants more from our relationship, more intimacy, and more commitment. Perhaps he has sensed, even before I did, that I was feeling some reservations. Yes, I bet that's it. That's why he's so reluctant to say anything about his own feelings. He's afraid of being rejected.

And Roger is thinking, *I'm going to have them look at the transmission again. I don't care what those morons say; it's still not shifting right. They better not try to blame it on the cold weather this time. What cold weather? It's 87 degrees and this thing is shifting like a garbage truck, and I paid those incompetent thieves $600.*

Elaine continues to think, *He's angry. And I don't blame him. I'd be angry, too. I feel so guilty, putting him through this, but I can't help the way I feel.*

I'm just not sure.

At this point, Roger is thinking, *They'll probably say it's only a ninety day warranty...idiots.*

And Elaine is thinking, *Maybe I'm just too idealistic, waiting for a knight to come riding up on his white horse, when I'm sitting right next to a perfectly good person, a person I enjoy being with, a person I truly do care about, a person who seems to truly care about me. A person who is in pain because of my self-centered, schoolgirl romantic fantasy.*

Roger is now thinking: *Warranty? They'd better not say it's only a ninety day warranty.*

"Roger," Elaine says aloud.

"What?" Roger replies startled.

"Please don't torture yourself like this," she says, her eyes beginning to brim with tears. "Maybe I should never have... Oh my, I feel so... She breaks down, sobbing.

"What?" says Roger without a clue.

"I'm such a fool," Elaine sobs. "I mean, I know there's no knight. I really know that. It's silly. There's no knight, and there's no horse."

"There's no horse?" asks Roger.

"You think I'm a fool, don't you?" Elaine says.

"No!" says Roger, glad to finally know the correct answer.

"It's just that...it's that I...I need some time," Elaine explains.

There is a fifteen second pause while Roger, thinking as fast as he can, tries to come up with a safe response. Finally he comes up with one he thinks might work. "Yes," he says.

Elaine, deeply moved, touches his hand. "Oh, Roger, do you really feel that way?" she says.

"What way?" Roger asks.

"That way about time," Elaine clarifies.

"Oh," says Roger. "Yes."

Elaine turns to face him and gazes deeply into his eyes, causing him to become nervous about what she might say next, especially if it involves a horse. At last she speaks.

"Thank you, Roger," she says softly.

"Thank you," says Roger in return.

Then he takes her home, and she lies on her bed, a conflicted, tortured soul, and weeps until dawn.

When Roger gets back to his place, he opens a bag of Doritos, turns on the TV, and immediately becomes deeply involved in a rerun of a tennis match between two Czechoslovakians he never heard of. A tiny voice in the far recesses of his mind tells him that something major was going on back there in the car, but he is pretty sure there is no way he would ever understand what, and so he figures it's better if he doesn't think about it. The next day Elaine will call her closest friend, or perhaps two of them, and they will talk about this situation for six straight hours. In painstaking detail, they will analyze everything she said and everything he said, going over it time and time again, exploring every word, expression, and gesture for nuances of meaning, considering every possible ramification.

CHAPTER FIVE

They will continue to discuss this subject, off and on, for weeks, maybe months, never reaching any definite conclusions, but never getting bored with it, either.

Meanwhile, Roger, while playing racquetball one day with a mutual friend of his and Elaine's, will pause just before serving, frown, and say, "Norm, did Elaine ever own a horse?"

And that's the difference between men and women!

TELL ME WHAT YOU DON'T LIKE
ABOUT YOURSELF!

On the popular FX cable network show Nip and Tuck, fictional plastic surgeons Troy and McNamara ask their patients who are contemplating going under the knife to:

"Tell me what don't you like about yourself?"

Whether it's her boobs that are too small or too large, or he needs a little or a lot of lipo around his stomach, patients describe their physical flaws. In getting ready to emotionally say I do, again, there may also be behavior, habits or traits that you don't like about yourself. Consider the following:

❧ DO YOU HAVE AN ADDICTIVE BEHAVIOR?
Are you a smoker?
Are you really trying to quit?
Do you drink too much?
Do you use illicit drugs?
Do you scream instead of talk?
Are you verbally abusive?
Are you physically abusive?

♛ HOW WOULD YOU DESCRIBE YOUR PERSONALITY?

Are you bitchy?

Do you complain about everything?

Are you unfriendly?

Do you not care?

Do you only care about yourself?

Are you jealous of other's good fortunes?

Are you insensitive?

Are you a liar?

As stated in Chapter One, the odds of a successful marriage the second time around are stacked up against you. That is not to say you can't improve your chances by recognizing now what you need to improve before you say I do, again.

MARGOT'S STORY— "BITCHY RICH GIRL"

Margot seemed to have it all; rich parents, went to an Ivy League school, was given a convertible sports car as a college graduation gift, and had an endless wardrobe of clothes. Along with being born with a silver spoon in her mouth, she was a bitch. In fact, if I can rate the one client who was the most obnoxious, it would be Margot.

My firm represented Margot in her first divorce which lasted less than two years. Not surprisingly, she retained our services for her second divorce which lasted half the length of her first marriage. When I came into the picture, she was about to say I do for a third time. Her Daddy, tired of "giving away the farm" insisted that Margot not marry without a pre-nuptial agreement. As the new guy in the firm, I was assigned the Margot file. Upon review, I called(her) to her make an appointment which proved difficult as she was always "too busy."

When we finally did meet, she was rudely late, did not offer any apology and barely made eye contact with me except to say that she was in my office only because, "Daddy made her go and she didn't want to risk losing her inheritance."

If you are bitchy, or have any other offensive personality, don't wait but do something about it now. No doubt, if you have money or looks you(will) find someone to remarry. But don't expect that wedding ring to be affixed to your finger forever. No matter how much money you may have, no one wants to live with someone whose persona is so toxic to herself and everyone she surrounds.

♛ ACCEPTING THE BRUTAL, HONEST TRUTH ABOUT YOU

As an attorney, I am trained to separate emotion from logic. If I did not, I would not be able to perform my job. As such, I am able to strip away what he said and she said, and filter out the nagging, name calling, and insults that often occur during a divorce. As it has been said time and time again, there is her story and then there is his. Somewhere in between lies, the brutally, honest truth.

That being said, your first marriage failed for a reason and a part of that reason was because of you. Yes, he may have cheated, drank too much, or was verbally abusive. Any of this type of behavior should not be condoned. However, some blame may be attributed to you. Were you an enabler? Did you ignore his cry for help? Until you accept some blame, you are not emotionally ready for remarriage.

PRACTICAL POINT: You may not agree with everything that is written in this book and you may even be offended by some of the things. Perhaps no one before has ever been as direct with you. Regardless, before you begin thinking about saying I do again, you need to accept the brutal, honest truth about you.

♛ WERE YOU/ARE YOU TOO CRITICAL?

Why are hurricanes named after women?

Because when they arrive, they're wet and wild. But when they go, they take your house and car.

Were you too critical of your spouse and that was a contributing factor to the marriage failing? No one likes to be told that everything they do is wrong and only your way is the right way. Accordingly, when assessing your personality, one of the questions that must be asked is whether your criticism of your Ex was warranted or whether it is your nature to be overly critical. If it is the latter, now is the time to leave that part of your personality behind before your next spouse says I don't.

You are too critical if:

- You never had problems getting dates, but for everyone you ever dated, there was always something about him that annoyed you to the point where you could not tolerate it.
- You have very specific ideas about who your partner needs to be which may include his religious and political views, income level, profession, and interests.
- You need a spouse to be constantly proving himself to you over and over again.

JOE'S STORY

Joe and Beverly were high school sweethearts. Joe went to UCLA on a football scholarship but was injured in his second year and had to drop out of the sports program. With a career in football behind him, he completed his major in marketing and upon graduation secured a job as a sales person for a pharmaceutical company.

When the two married, Beverly kept telling her family and friends that Joe would eventually apply to law school. But after five years, he was enjoying his work and going back to school was the last thing on his mind. However, Beverly only saw herself being married to a lawyer and openly told her friends that a salesman would never make enough money to satisfy her needs. After two years of insults that he would never amount to anything, the parties divorced.

After thirty years of marriage, I have endured as much criticism as any other husband as my wife still reminds me that I leave the bathroom a mess after showering or I don't load the dishwasher properly. Even though I have heard her say these things for the duration of our marriage, they are not hateful or hurtful, and just go with the territory of being married. However, a person who has to live day after day with someone who constantly reminds them they do not meet her standards has the air sucked out of the marriage and will eventually terminate the relationship.

Accordingly, in the bigger overall picture of a successful marriage, the following is what you should be critical of. The rest is just not that important:

- ***Qualities that will matter in the long run: a similar value system, communication style, and level of integrity***

    Ensuring your potential partners have these same qualities makes being in the relationship with each other easier—the two of you will be on the same page in many aspects.

- *Your partner should have the same family goals as you*
- *You want someone with the same family goals because they can be relationship breakers if you're not in agreement.*
- *Choosing a kind and gentle person who cares about people's emotions*

    Relationships can be hard. In hard times you want a partner who will treat you well instead of poorly.

- *Choosing a person who has no Exes lurking around hoping to reignite the relationship*

    Lurking Ex spouses tend to cause problems for relationships because the lurked on is often torn between the past and present relationship and cannot fully be in either.

- *The person you choose should have a job or even a career, and his or her life and finances in order, or at least be working on it*

    You want someone who is living well with or without you to avoid unhealthy dependencies and resentments.

- *The person should be someone you enjoy looking at and someone you find attractive*

    Healthy physical intimacy is critical to a long-term, happy relationship. Without a mutual attraction, this is something you will not have.

♛ ARE YOU MATURE ENOUGH TO GET MARRIED AGAIN?

If you have been sheltered by your family, cannot make decisions for yourself, and depend on others, you still need some growing up to do before you can say I do, again. To illustrate, if you grew up with a Mom and Dad who expressed love for each other, your observations will help you in your second marriage. If you are the product of a divorce where your Mom or Dad were always ragging on their Ex, you may have brought this negative behavior into your first marriage. If so, before you tie the knot again, you need to rid yourself of anything negative associated with your prior marriage.

♛ ARE YOU FINANCIALLY SECURE?

Unless your name is Bill Gates, no one can ever have enough money. It is important that you have enough money to survive. You should not enter into a remarriage if money is the motivating factor. Likewise, you should not get married if marrying your fiancé will put you in debt. Please see Chapter Thirteen for a further discussion.

❦ ARE YOU OUT TO WIN OR ARE YOU A TEAM PLAYER

To make a marriage work, both spouses must be willing to compromise. It cannot always go your way! Before you say I do, again, consider the battles you lost in your first marriage and analyze whether you fought them on the principal that you always had to win. If so, understand that a successful remarriage is not about only winning and losing. As long as your team is happy, you are a winner.

❦ ARE YOU A MAGNET FOR LOSERS?

A woman applying for a job at a lemon packaging company seemed over qualified for the position. "Look miss," said the foreman, "have you had any experience picking lemons?" "Well, as a matter of fact, yes," she replied. "I've been divorced three times."

In getting ready to say I do, again, analyze the type of person who is attracted to you. Have you only dated aging rock and rollers who are still working on their first album? Perhaps all of the men in your life sought you out not only because you are beautiful, sweet, and kind, but also because you believed in them when no one else would. Maybe it was this attraction to you that made you attracted to him.

STEPHANIE'S STORY

Stephanie married her first husband right after high school. He was trying to start his band which finally disbanded along with her six month marriage. Husband number two was a starving poet who spent his days submitting proposals for greeting cards to Hallmark. Stephanie could not afford to lose any more weight and said goodbye to Edgar Alan Poe. Husband number three was a salesman by day and a drummer by night. During their eight year marriage where she worked two jobs and raised two children while Ringo beat his head against the wall auditioning for a gig. Finally, with two kids to raise and single again, Stephanie thought she finally met the man who would be the answer to all of her prayers. Enter Fred, a consultant to the payphone industry. Fred seemed to have it all; a house, a car, and a big screen TV. He also shared his home with multiple glasses of red ruby wine every night to drink himself into oblivion. Stephanie, at age fifty, was now single again!

Sure you have to feel sorry for Stephanie. But in speaking with her, she admitted that each guy was so convincing that they "were going to make it" and only needed her support. Eager to help, she took on the project only to see it fail over and over again.

♛ ARE YOU ATTRACED TO THE UNDERDOG?

Did you marry your Ex because you felt sorry for him? Are you attracted to the underdog? Many times it is the type of person you are attracted to that lays the foundation for another failed marriage.

IRENE'S STORY

Irene was married when she was eighteen years old soon after she graduated high school. That marriage lasted only two years as she said he had all these wild dreams but could not hold down a job.

Her next husband was an "entrepreneur" which sometimes is a fancy word to describe someone who does not want to work for others and instead is pursuing a product or invention that will make him richer than Bill Gates. Irene worked two jobs to support her husband and their two small children. Throughout the nine year marriage, while her husband bounced around from job to job always saying that he was on the verge of hitting it big.

When she married for the third time, she said it felt different. Her husband to be was fifteen years older than she, was a national sales manager, had some money in the bank, and most important he liked her kids. After only two years, he announced that he was tired of working while his boss got rich from his efforts. He abruptly quit his job saying they would have to "survive off his savings and when that was gone, he would worry about his next move."

Irene's story is more common than you think. As a little girl, she was the child who came home with the stray cat or dog. That is not to say you should not feel sorry for an animal who is lost or hurt, or the nice guy at work whose parents were tragically killed in an auto accident. As adults, we have presumably grown up. Regardless, you should never confuse feeling sorry with feelings of love.

Walk Slowly to the Altar

I n every relationship there are assigned tasks. Now that you are flying solo again, you are finding yourself having to do what you have already done and more. In order to be emotionally ready to say I do, again, a sufficient amount of time should pass between when you say I don't and the next time you say I do. Consider the following:

Ann's Story

Ann married soon after graduating college but after five years, she and her husband realized they were going in different directions. Though they had a beautiful daughter, Ann was on the fast track at work and he was content with an hourly wage desk job with no room for advancement. Their divorce was amicable and within weeks of separating, Ann was dating again.

By the time her divorce was final she had met Bill. He had never been married, was a few years older than Ann, and loved children. He was also "Mr. Fixit" around the house which was a big help to Ann as she was dependent on someone to replace her Ex.

Unfortunately, the benefits of having a handyman were clearly outweighed by the detriments of living with an alcoholic as Bill could not control his drinking and Ann soon found herself in our office for a second time.

There is no self-help book or guide that will tell you how long you should wait after a divorce before you give serious thought about walking down the aisle a second time. I have read books that suggest one or two years, maybe even longer. Only you can decide this. Regardless, as in any major life event, time is the greatest healer. You will know when it is the right time.

♛ YOU DON'T NEED TO GET IT RIGHT, JUST BETTER!
How often have you heard someone who has been divorced say:

"I am going to get it right the next time."

It is not necessarily a matter of getting it right the second time around. Give yourself a free pass that perhaps the first time the thought of getting married overshadowed what it meant to be married. Perhaps too much detail was given to the invitations and the dress, and the idea of being married. Now that all the excitement of a first marriage is behind you, greater detail must be placed on making it better.

SPECIAL SITUATION: WANTING TO REMARRY BECAUSE YOUR BIOLOGICAL CLOCK IS TICKING?

For obvious reasons that do not require a science background to understand, if you want to have a family there is more pressure placed on a woman. As a result, your biological time clock sometimes gets confused with the clock beating in your chest resulting in a marriage for the wrong reason.

RHONDA'S STORY

Rhonda married when she was twenty and was divorced at age twenty-eight. After several relationships that never seem to go anywhere, she looked at the calendar and realized that she would soon be celebrating her thirtieth birthday. While many of her friends had started families, she was alone with no prospects on the horizon.

Enter Jason. Jason had never been married and his online profile read that he was looking for a "long-term relationship, marriage, and children. At the ripe old age of thirty-two, he was ready to settle down with Mrs. Right. Rhonda and Jason dated for six months when he popped the question. But as soon as the preacher pronounced them husband and wife, Rhonda wanted to get down to the business of making babies. This, however, was not on the top of Jason's agenda as he wanted to slowly ease into the idea of starting a family and first enjoy life as husband and wife before any little ones were sharing Sunday morning in bed with them.

Eventually, the issue of starting a family overshadowed their entire married life. Finally, Rhonda gave Jason an ultimatum wrongfully believing that he would give in. To her surprise, he announced that the marriage was over.

✿ HE MAY NOT BE MR. RIGHT, BUT HE IS MR. RIGHT NOW!"

At the cocktail party, one woman said to another, "Aren't you wearing your wedding ring on the wrong finger?" The other woman replied, "Yes I am. I married the wrong man."

When shopping for a new kitchen appliance, would you rather buy the latest stainless steel model or last year's avocado green that has a small factory dent on the side that only you will see? Thinking about getting remarried again is a lot like buying that appliance. Of course you are in love again or at least think you are. There may even be a ring at the end of the rainbow. But before you consider saying I do again, you must analyze whether you are settling for "Mr. Right Now" instead of "Mr. Right." If he is the former, chances are your future will be filled with the same unhappiness you encountered in your first marriage.

✿ REASONS WHY IT IS EASY TO SETTLE

Have you ever had this discussion with yourself?

• When I was first married, all of my friends were getting married. It was the thing to do. Now, everyone I know is married and I am again single. I don't like the title and want to rejoin the club of married people.

• Financially, things were better when I was married. It is more expensive to survive as one.

• My life is stalled; I can't seem to move forward.

- This person seems to really like me and I don't want an opportunity to pass me by.

- I am not getting any younger.

- I don't want to die alone.

- You are approaching dating as if it were a term paper. That is you have a deadline and you must meet Mr. Right by a certain date.

- You have dated for so long that you are exhausted and are willing to settle for the first guy who proposes.

- You want to get off the dating merry-go-round.

You should never say I do, again because there is this nice person who has asked you to marry him. Sure, you are older than when you first married and your life has evolved. Perhaps you now have children, more financial obligations, or think you are not as desirable as you were before. Though these may be valid concerns, simply because he has asked for your hand in marriage is not enough.

Accordingly, before you say I do, again, ask yourself the following questions.

1. Are you fearful that if you say no, you will never have another chance to get remarried?
2. Is there someone else in the wings that he might pursue if you say no?
3. Has your self-esteem decreased? Do you really think you can't do any better?
4. Has he been so kind and caring to you that you fear hurting his feelings?
5. Though you recognize problems between the two of you, do you really believe they will improve once you are married?
6. Are you tired of living alone?
7. Have you given more thought to breaking up than getting married?

☙ ARE YOU ON THE DATING MERRY-GO-ROUND?

If you have ever taken a European vacation where you visited more countries than days that you were there, you will probably never do that again. The real way to learn about a country is to spend quality time there.

Similarly, if you are out there dating, and each weekend it is a new name and face, after a while it gets tiring though you want to meet someone whom you can establish a quality relationship with. However, wanting to get off the dating merry-go-round, you may find yourself settling by saying I do again. But remarrying just for the sake of being married, does not guarantee that you will achieve the happiness you deserve to have in your life.

FACTOID! Statistically, most persons who remarry do so within seven years after their divorce. However, statistics are just that. Unless the time is right for you, you should not feel pressured by the passage of time to say I do, again.

☙ MARRYING FOR A QUICK FIX

Remarriage does not automatically fix any problems you may have had during your first marriage. If there were reasons why you were not happy, unrelated to your spouse, it is unrealistic for you to think that remarriage will change things. Furthermore, it is not fair to this new person to enter into a relationship knowing he or she will be unhappy due to your problems.

ANN'S AND IAN'S STORY

Ann was married for nine years when her husband sought a divorce. Ann disclosed that she had suffered from depression which manifested after the tragic death of her parents from a car accident. She did seek counseling during the marriage but it was not enough to fix things.

She waited two years after her divorce to start dating again and was taking medication for her depression when she met Ian. He had never been married before. After a few dates, she confided in him about her mental problem but he said that, "he would try to help her work through it." Buoyed by Ian's kind words, Ann accepted his proposal to marry hoping he would be the cure for her depression.

Unfortunately, Ian was not the magic pill and Ann's depression worsened after marriage. She would not answer the ringing phone or the knock on the front door. She also spent many of her weekdays in bed and did not always shower. Though her doctors increased her medication, Ann drifted further and further away from Ian and her world finally taking her life by overdosing.

♛ WARNING SIGNS THAT YOU MAY BE LOOKING FOR A QUICK FIX

- Do you see other people laughing and having a good time and wonder why that can't be you?

- Does your life seem boring?

- Do you dwell on the time when you were married and look upon everything that occurred after your divorce as "going downhill?"

- Do you have a mental issue that has not been fully addressed?

- Do you have an addictive behavior?

- Do you feel troubled or lonely?

- Are you without a good friend to confide in?

- Do you depend on others to provide your happiness?

- Do you bury your head in the sand ignoring taking responsibility for your actions?

- Do you see marrying again the answer to all of your problems?

♛ WHEN IT'S WRONG TO REMARRY

Do you feel like a half gallon of milk sitting on a shelf in the refrigeration section of your supermarket bearing an expiration date that states it must be sold before time runs out? Is your expiration date to remarry quickly approaching?

Many of our clients reported that they felt compelled to remarry. One client even remarked that she felt like she had an incurable disease because she did not remarry. The timing of remarriage has to be right for you. Sure, it will please your parents and friends. But it is your happiness that matters most.

RANDY'S STORY

Randy was very attractive and enjoying her career as a buyer for a major department store. But Randy's mother was not as happy. She constantly reminded her that she was over thirty and divorced, and that her window to ever meet someone again was quickly closing. Along with the lecture came the motherly message that, "Her eggs were not getting any younger."

Pressured by her over bearing parent, Randy accepted a date that was arranged by her Mom's match making friend. Mark was tall, good looking, and never married. The first date went okay enough for Randy to accept another date with Mark. Meanwhile, her mother began in her mind planning the wedding.

Randy and Mark dated for almost six months when they both decided there was not enough going on between them to take the relationship to the next level. Randy's mother was predictably mortified and now convinced that her daughter would become an old maid and she would never enjoy being a grandmother.

Randy was able to withstand the pressure from her mother and two years later did meet Mr. Right. Today, she and her husband are raising two beautiful children. But not everyone is as strong in mind as Randy. Accordingly, before you say I do, again, do so for you and not someone else!

♛ POINTS AND COUNTERPOINTS TO REMARRIAGE

At one time, The CBS program 60 Minutes had a segment where two commentators took opposing positions on a subject and debated each other. The person making the counter argument was known as Rebuttal. The following are common positions that favor remarriage and how you might respond in rebuttal:

- ***You're the odd man out as all of your friends are married.***
  This may be true but are they all happily married?
- ***Your parents will not rest until they see you married again.***
  Remind them of how painful your divorce was and ask them if they really want to see that tale unravel again.

- ***Your children need two parents in the home.***

  Depending upon your children's ages, you may want to remind them what life was like in the home with Mom and Dad.
- ***You think about remarriage but have not met anyone yet.***

  Embrace your newly awarded status as a single person.
- ***You feel you are missing the boat.***

  Statistically there are countless persons who are divorced and are in the same boat as you. Besides, new boats are being built every year.

MAYBE YOU'RE BETTER OFF NOT MARRYING AGAIN

First guy proudly proclaims, "My wife's an angel."
Second guy responds, "You're lucky. Mine's still alive!"

Are you the marrying type? Was it a mistake to get married the first time? These are tough questions. Before you consider a second trip down the aisle, you must be confident in your answers. Remarrying because someone else says you should will almost always lead to marriage failure.

In researching for this book, my clients cited many reasons why they would not marry again. But the most common were:

❦ YOU ARE HAPPIER BEING SINGLE

Coming out of a very terrible marriage that was filled with anger and hate, it is only logical that someone may prefer to be single. If married life made yours too difficult, then you may want to think again before considering his proposal. Do not feel that your family and friends will look upon you as being selfish. Remember, it is your life!

❦ HAVING A FAMILY IS NOT IN YOUR CARDS

From a biblical sense, marriage is all about procreation. If you do not have children, have never seen yourself as wanting them, and feel you are being pressured by family or friends to get on the bandwagon and have kids, these are the wrong reasons to get married again.

❦ YOU TRIED IT ONCE AND IT DID NOT WORK

Some people who have divorced recognize marriage as a failure. Despite the reasons for the divorce, they do not want to associate themselves with a subsequent failure. In others words, once was enough and the fear of failing again is enough to scare you away from the altar. Again, do not surrender to the pressures of family, friends, or society.

⫻ FACTOID! According to the United States Census Bureau, 10 percent
⫻ of adults never get married. Out of those that do and later divorce, 20
⫻ percent never get remarried.

HOW MARRIAGE CHANGES A RELATIONSHIP

A friend of mine sent me this joke. It is purportedly e-mail correspondence between a frustrated software user and tech support. Aside from the humor, there is a lot said that may be very true. Accordingly, before you think remarriage, consider the tech support person's response to the desperate software user.

Re: INSTALLING HUSBAND 2.0.

> Dear Tech Support,

> Last year I upgraded from Boyfriend 5.0 to New Husband 2.0. Note,
  years ago I used Husband 1.0 on my old computer but I deleted it as
  it was constantly crashing and it was not compatible with my other
  programs.
With Husband 2.0, I noticed a distinct slowdown in overall system
performance, particularly
> in the flower and jewelry applications, which operated flawlessly un-
  der Boyfriend 5.0.
>
> In addition, Husband 2.0 uninstalled many other valuable pro-
grams, such as Romance 9.5 and Personal Attention 6.5, and then
installed undesirable programs such as: NBA 5. 0, NFL 3.0, and Golf
Clubs 4.1.
>
> Conversation 8.0 no longer runs, and Housecleaning 2.6 simply
> crashes the system.
>
> Please note that I have tried running Nagging 5.3 to fix these
> problems, but to no avail.

> What can I do?
> Signed, Desperate.
>
>
> DEAR DESPERATE,
> First, keep in mind, Boyfriend 5.0 is an Entertainment Package, while Husband 2.0 is an operating system similar to Husband 1.0 which Husband 2.0 replaced.
> Please enter command: ithoughtyoulovedme.html and try to download Tears 6.2 and do not forget to install the Guilt 3.0 update. If that application works as designed, Husband 2.0 should then automatically run the applications Jewelry 2.0 and Flowers 3.5.
> However, remember that overuse of the above application can cause Husband 2.0 to default to Grumpy Silence 2.5, Happy Hour 7.0, or
> Beer 6.1. Please note that Beer 6.1 is a very bad program that will
> download the Farting and Snoring Loudly Beta.
> Whatever you do, DO NOT under any circumstances install
> Mother-In-Law 2.0 (it runs a virus in the background that will
> eventually seize control of all your system resources.)
> In addition, please do not attempt to reinstall the Boyfriend 5.0. These are unsupported applications and will crash Husband 2.0.
>
> In summary, Husband 2.0 is a great program, but it does have
> limited memory and cannot learn new applications quickly. You might consider buying additional software to improve memory and performance.
> We recommend: Cooking 3.0 and Hot Lingerie 7.7.
>
> Good Luck Babe!
> Tech Support

REMARRYING FOR LOVE OR MONEY

Are you remarrying for money? We have all heard the expression "money does not bring happiness."
Bull! I have yet to meet anyone who feels depressed to count his money.

After a divorce, even if all the assets are equally divided, it still costs more to survive as a single person than when you were married. What's more for you women, you may actually be happier after your divorce now that your Ex is out of your everyday life. Statistics show that you are probably a lot poorer. This is especially true if you did not work outside your home while you raised your children, as reentering the workforce often requires that you learn new skills and will generally earn less money than your male counterparts.

With less money available and the same if not more bills to pay, I have witnessed many women driven to the altar for a second time only because that new person in their life can offer you the financial support and lifestyle that you were accustomed to during your first marriage. However, money alone should not be the motivating factor for you to say I do, again. Consider the following:

♛ I NEED TO FEED THE KIDS

Sadly, a child support order is often only worth the paper it is written on. Though many states have strengthened the laws enforcing child support orders by allowing for the attachment of government benefits and suspending driving privileges for those who violate a support order,   many of our clients find themselves dependent upon support checks that are always late and often not enough to provide for their children's needs.

As a result, a single Mom who has reentered the dating world often discovers, "Mr. Checkbook" He may or may not be attractive. But he seems to like your kids and he pays for dinner and treats everyone to the movies. He even brings birthday presents for little Jack and Jill. Ask yourself, is Mr. Checkbook the right book for you? Are you remarrying for financial survival instead of for love?

♛ I USED TO HAVE CLEANING HELP BUT NOW I WASH MY OWN SHEETS!

Does it sound shallow that a client complains that she use to afford cleaning help in her house but now has to wash her own sheets? Or that she has a standing appointment every week to have her nails done? Or that she can no longer afford her personal trainer? I guess it does. But when you are married, the income from the marriage affords a husband and wife to live a certain lifestyle. In those fortunate marriages where there was always discretionary income after the bills were paid, you were able to pamper yourself If your Ex was ordered to pay you alimony, the purpose of such an order is to allow you to continue living the lifestyle you were accustomed to.

Sometimes in a divorce, the court will take into account that your Ex now has expenses that did not exist during the marriage. For example, he has to live somewhere so there is the additional cost of housing. He may need to finance another car, buy furniture for where he lives, and so on. As a result, his paycheck that may have allowed the two of you to enjoy a nice life together as husband and wife is not big enough to allow each of you separately the same life. A solution, but not always the correct one, is to marry someone who can keep you in the lifestyle you were accustomed to.

LEGALLY SPEAKING! If you are now receiving alimony, your remarriage will terminate those benefits. Accordingly, proceed cautiously into remarriage as your future financial situation can become even more perilous if the second time around goes bust!

♛ ARE YOU TRYING TO CATCH UP FOR LOST TIME?

So your first marriage was for love. While all of your married girlfriends were showing off their fancy cars, decorating their homes, and shopping till they dropped, your husband often worked two jobs just to provide the basics. Then the marriage ended leaving you without ever experiencing the luxury vacation, the BMW in the garage, and the closet filled with shoes you will never wear. Now divorced, you feel it is your turn to live the good life.

Well, it's great to think you can catch up for lost time and live the life-style of the rich and famous. You must also accept that you are now a few years older and those size six jeans hanging in the closet are tighter to get on than they once were.

To make matters worse, your competition is even greater than you ever imagined as you are not only competing with other women your age but with those even younger than you are. If you don't believe this as fact, consider a study conducted by the online dating service, Match.com. Their research shows that men who are seeking to remarry are looking for a woman who is at least ten years younger. In fact, there is even a guideline for determining that age. Simply take his age, divide by two and add twelve years. Therefore a fifty-four-year-old man can be seen with a thirty-nine-year-old woman and society will not question the age difference. Unfortunately society is not as understanding for women.

♛ REMARRYING BECAUSE "I DESERVE IT!"

When a woman discovers that her husband has been having an affair, she feels betrayed. But when she learns of the lavish gifts that "their" money was used to buy for the "other woman," she wants revenge. In states that require a showing of fault, a cheating spouse may not be entitled to an equal division of the marital assets. As such, the innocent spouse got her revenge in court. But so called "no fault states," do not care who was cheating with whom with marital assets being divided equally.

LEGALLY SPEAKING! If you reside in a community property state, the divorce court will only order that all assets and liabilities be equally divided if both sides cannot agree to a division. Therefore, do not assume everything has to be divided 50/50.

PRACTICAL POINT: It is not uncommon for a non cheating spouse to feel that she was cheated out of what was hers during the marriage. Acting on this resentment, she will search out a second husband who can buy her those things she deserves. Too often, however, she will quickly discover that material objects are not a substitute for true love.

♛ ARE YOU ATTRACTED TO HIM OR HIS MONEY?

Before you say I do, again, question your motives. The following is a checklist of questions to ask yourself:

- Are you having serious financial problems?
- Is the amount you receive for support unable to pay your bills?
- Are you being hounded by creditors and see no way out?
- Do you feel desperate and are overwhelmed by your finances?
- Did you have to radically lower your living standards after your divorce?
- Are you dating someone only because he has money?

For a more complete discussion about your financial issues, please see Chapter Fourteen.

HOW TO HANDLE LONELINESS

Being married affords sharing life's experiences with someone. Whether it is going out to dinner or a simple night home in front of the TV, you are not alone.

Of course, after the legal wrangling and emotions of a divorce have subsided, the loneliness that follows divorce can be difficult. There are only so many dinners that your friends who feel sorry will invite you to. Unless you want to bury yourself in your home or apartment and not have a life, you must accept the fact that you are that person going to the movies on a Saturday night and purchasing one ticket. So much for ordering the combo popcorn and large Coke!

SATISFYING YOUR NEEDS

♛ IS IT LOVE OR COMPANIONSHIP YOU ARE SEEKING?
- Do you want a relationship because you can't live alone?
- Have you never lived alone and are scared to do it now?
- Have you always had a boyfriend in your life?
- Do you obsess about being lonely?
- Do your friends and family tell you that you need your independence?
- Are you too dependent on friends and family to make decisions?

Satisfying your desire to not be alone can easily be confused with seeking companionship. Believe it or not, being alone again does have benefits. It allows you the time to clear your thoughts and transition from your married life to being single again.

However, for most people who have been married before, statistics show that they are very eager to get back on the horse and try marriage again. But let's face it. Do you really want to go on a vacation by yourself? Don't you feel weird laughing to Curb Your Enthusiasm with no one in the room to share your laughter?

Before you grab the first person with a beating heart and race down the aisle, you must ask yourself , are you marrying for love or companionship. Love comes with companionship but companionship does not guarantee love. Consider the following.

LORRAINE'S STORY

Lorraine was forty-five and had been divorced for more than twelve years. She was fed up with the dating scene. She daydreamed about one day exploring Europe with someone special and was depressed from coming home to her empty apartment. Lorraine loved to cook and had amassed a huge collection of cookbooks but had no one to prepare a gourmet meal for.

She decided to give an online dating service one more chance and began chatting with Brian. He was also divorced. When they eventually met, they had a lot in common. For Lorraine, it was a welcomed change to go to a sit down restaurant as opposed to a fast food chain. She also impressed Brian with her culinary talents. Though her heart did not stop when she would think about him, the thought of being alone for the rest of her life was downright depressing.

Within a few weeks of dating, she was already telling her friends that "Brian was the one." Though he was not as anxious as her, he saw the financial benefits of marriage and six months later they were married. Unfortunately, Lorraine had not taken the time to get to know Brian before she said I do, again (he was) as hewas verbally abusive and overly possessive. Lorraine related that she felt as though she was suffocating when she was with him. Ashamed, she admitted to her friends that she had failed in marriage again and was seeking a divorce.

Lorraine's rush to the altar was as a result of her confusion between wanting to be married and not wanting to be alone.

♛ ONE DOES NOT HAVE TO BE THE LONELIEST NUMBER

In the movie, *War of the Roses* starring Michael Douglas and Kathleen Turner, their marriage got so bad that they literally divided the house preventing either one of them from crossing the dividing line. As bad as things were for the Roses', they were still a couple until a divorce court ordered otherwise.

If you have been married for a short period of time, it is probably an easier adjustment for you to once again be single. However, the longer that you were married, adjusting to living as one can be most challenging. As a result, there is an urgency to turn the number one into two.

However, you are not alone as, according to the United States Census Bureau, there are over thirty-eight million divorced and widowed adults living in the United States. So before you throw a pity party for yourself, consider the fact there are lots of other wonderful people out there rediscovering their single lives.

Until you are secure in being single again, you are not ready to enter a serious relationship with the prospect of marriage. Instead, if you act impulsively just to fill the void of loneliness, you may be setting yourself up for making the same mistakes all over again.

PRACTICAL POINT: The past is the past and the future has just begun. So, before you jump into another relationship, chart your future. If you were not busy before, get involved now. There are people who need your help. Volunteer. Get involved. Throw out any lessons you were taught by your family about dating. It is okay to approach someone to ask them out. If you absolutely cannot deal with being alone, adopt a dog or cat. A pet is a lot cheaper and they provide unconditional love with no strings attached.

LEGALLY SPEAKING! Job, credit, and many other types of applications ask for your marital status. Each time you check "single," it serves as a constant reminder to you of your previous marriage. However, the court has restored your status as single so start using it.

ADDICTED TO SEX OR ADDICTED TO LOVE

Companionship means different things to different people. For many, it is the desire of not wanting to be alone. As a product of marriage, it includes the availability of sex on demand. Often, however, persons who are addicted to sex rather than love find that marriage is not their answer.

ARE YOU ADDICTED TO LOVE?

MTV's most requested video of all-time was Robert Palmer's Addicted to Love. The video featured him with four remarkably beautiful and scantily clad women singing:

- *Your lights are on, but you're not home*
- *Your mind is not your own*
- *Your heart sweats, your body shakes*
- *Another kiss is what it takes*
- *You can't sleep, you can't eat*
- *There's no doubt, you're in deep*
- *Your throat is tight, you can't breathe*
- *Another kiss is all you need . . . because you are addicted to love.*

Being in a relationship sure feels good; someone cares for you, admires you, respects you, and desires you. What could be better? For some, it is the need to be desired that may drive you at warped speed to the altar. In doing so, you go through every red light just to achieve the satisfaction of love that is waiting for you at the finish line.

Unfortunately, marriage is not built on love alone. Accordingly before you say I do, again, ask yourself the following:

- Do you require constant flattery?
- Are you easily romanced?
- Are you gullible and sincerely believe every kind word that is said to you?
- Does every person you meet immediately evolve into a serious relationship?
- Do you go from one relationship to the next with very little time in between?
- Do you excessively day dream about your next wedding?
- Have you misinterpreted having sex for being in love?
- Do you find yourself bragging to your friends about your sex life?

JESSICA'S STORY

Jessica was in love with herself and needed constant flattery. Her first marriage failed because she said her Ex did not give her enough attention in the bedroom. After her divorce, she dated several men but all of her relationships ended as quickly as they began.

When she met Kevin, there was an immediate attraction. She said he was as good looking as she was beautiful and always felt a sexual tension between the two of them. So, after a few months of dating, they ran off to Las Vegas to tie the knot.

Soon after returning home to begin life as a married couple, Kevin received a job promotion that required him to do traveling. This included a few days a month when he would be out of town. This became a problem for Jessica as she became sexually frustrated. As a result, she started having an affair with a co-worker which Kevin found out about. After confronting her, Jessica agreed to seek help for her sexual addiction but quickly relapsed finding love with another co-worker.

PRACTICAL POINT: At first blush, some readers may wish they were infected with Jessica's problem. But remarrying again solely to satisfy your sexual needs does not guarantee a successful remarriage.

✿ REMARRYING TO AVOID DATING FEAR

If you have had a long-term first marriage, just the idea that you now have to market yourself, let alone become physical with someone could be frightening. Dating fear is quite real, especially after a long marriage. Aside from physical concerns, (you may be a little or a lot heavier, you may have lost some or all of your hair) there is a tendency to feel that you will not be desirable to someone new. As a result, there may be an impulse to hook up with the first guy or gal who comes along that seems interesting.

ROBIN'S STORY

Robin married her high school sweetheart. They were married for twenty-nine years and had three daughters who were in college. She was blindsided when her husband announced that he was leaving her. She later found out he had been having an affair with his secretary.

Now, facing the idea of dating petrified her. She did, however, join an online dating service but was disappointed with the quality of the guys who responded to her. Finally, a girlfriend introduced her to Mike. He was also newly divorced and, after meeting for coffee, discovered they shared similar backgrounds.

Coffee led to dinner and then many dinner dates. Within a month, Robin was telling her friends that she had a strong feeling Mike was going to ask her to marry him. Her friends told her it was way too soon and she needed to date other guys. She replied that she was not getting any younger, was scared of the lunatics out there, and was willing to take a chance. Within a year, Robin was in our office filing for her second divorce. Had she been a betting person, she probably would have gotten better odds that her number would come up at a roulette table.

REMARRYING FOR REVENGE!

"When a woman steals your husband, there is no better revenge than to let her keep him."

D uring the initial consultation, it is quite common for a client to pour out her heart about what went wrong and what she should have done to change things. Oftentimes we have heard the following:

- *I hate his girlfriend and wish her harm*
- *I hope his girlfriend walks in front of a moving bus*
- *I will show him*
- *I will take him to the cleaners for every thing he is worth*

Regardless of who should take the blame for the divorce, it is logical to feel anger. You may be angry at yourself for allowing something to happen or angry at him for causing you such harm. However, you should not enter into a remarriage as a way of getting even with your Ex. If you do, you will be throwing logic out the window and making decisions based on your emotional impulses.

SANDY'S STORY

Sandy and Rick met in college and married when they graduated. They were both business majors and were successful in landing high paying jobs at different brokerage businesses upon graduation.

After five years of marriage, Sandy and Rick decided to start a family. Another five years later, they had three children and were living comfortably on Rick's salary as Sandy had now become a full-time stay-at-home Mom.

Rick continued to climb up the corporate ladder and by the tenth year of their marriage, he became a regional vice president. Likewise, Sandy and Rick's lifestyle also climbed as they joined a country club and the kids were enrolled in private schools. All seemed to be going great except that Rick could never take time off to go on a family vacation though he complained about all the weeks he spent during the year traveling for business. In the bedroom Rick seemed disinterested in sex though Sandy assumed he was stressed from his work.

For three more years Sandy continued to ignore these warning signs and thought they could make up for lost time when Rick agreed to go on a family cruise. The day before they were to leave, Rick announced to her that he had been involved for many years with another woman and that he was leaving her immediately.

Her divorce was very ugly and she could not cope with the fact that Rick had been cheating on her for so many years. Her emotional Richter scale went off the chart when her husband's attorney advised us that Rick was planning to remarry and asked if we would agree to have the marriage dissolved now and the remaining issues handled at a later time.

In hearing this news, all Sandy wanted was revenge and in less than six months we learned from a mutual friend that she was married in Las Vegas. Not surprisingly, the odds of success were overwhelming stacked against her and she soon appeared in our office seeking an annulment.

Before you say I do, again, ask yourself

- Are you getting remarried to get even with your Ex?
- Are you getting remarried to spite your Ex?
- Are you getting remarried to prove to your Ex that someone else finds you attractive?

- Are you getting married because your Ex has remarried?

If your answers to any of the above questions is yes, STOP the wedding plans and refocus on why you are about to walk down the aisle again.

PRACTICAL POINT: Do not transfer your feelings of hurt into wanting to get back at your Ex. This is not a game. Accept that the marriage is over and your next move is to meet someone who truly loves you.

♛ MARRYING ON THE REBOUND

Whether you have been divorced for months, years, or emotionally divorced for years, sooner or later, you will meet someone who appears interesting. He could be someone you already know but that you now look at in a different way. Or it could be someone you have met by chance. Regardless, don't let your emotions for wanting to meet someone blur your logic for needing to take your time.

TERESA'S STORY

I had said goodbye to Teresa outside the courtroom where minutes earlier we were before the judge finalizing her divorce. As we left, I directed her to the Office of Records as she wanted to pick up a copy of her birth certificate.

A few days later my secretary informed me that Teresa had called with a question and then told her she had met this cute guy in the clerk's office and they were going to have dinner. I laughed it off. But three months later Teresa was on the phone again informing me that she married this guy and now wanted to annul the marriage. When I asked her why she tied the knot again so soon, she answered,

"I'm just stupid."

Call it stupidity or marrying on the rebound. However you want to label it, WAIT until the ink dries on your divorce papers before you say I do, again.

SPECIAL SITUATION—REMARRIAGE AFTER THE DEATH OF YOUR SPOUSE

When a husband and wife exchange vows, the words "until death td us part" may be spoken but given little attention. Marrying the person of your dreams only to have your life shattered by his or her passing is probably one of the saddest of all life cycle events. When that person passes, for some the thought of ever marrying again is not a consideration as the grieving process never really ends.

Likewise, most persons don't want to spend the rest of their lives alone and the day may arrive when you meet someone whom you may consider for remarriage. However, until you have completed the grieving process, remarriage is not an option.

Furthermore, having been married before, you have memories of your spouse. Hopefully, if your marriage was good, your mind is filled with happy and loving thoughts. As such, it is common for persons, especially after a long-term marriage, to tell friends that

"I will never meet anyone who can replace my wife."

When suffering the loss of a loved one, the passing of time does not fade our memories. Instead it allows you the time to put your life into perspective so that you can move on, yet never forgetting the wonderful time you had with that person when he or she was here. Before committing to someone knew, ask yourself if this person is simply filling a void in your life?

PRACTICAL POINT: Statistics reveal that three out of four people who remarry after a divorce usually do so within three years. Many widowers, especially men, get quickly involved in a relationship after the death of their spouse. Is this a rebound relationship? Maybe, especially considering you lost someone who you shared a significant part of your life with. While there's no exact time limit for remarriages, it's in your best interest and the interest of the relationship to take your time. Not only do you have to accept the loss of a loved one, you must be able to reconcile your emotions with what happened in order to have a new, healthy relationship. A solid marriage also means getting to know someone, and that doesn't happen in a matter of months.

CHAPTER ELEVEN

♛ A CHECKLIST FOR REMARRYING AFTER THE LOSS OF A SPOUSE

- ***Before committing to someone new, consider your kids***

  If you have children, take the time to help them get to know this new person. Don't take their acceptance for granted! Depending on their ages they will have different reactions.

- ***Lose the notion that you are cheating on your spouse by dating again.***

  You are not looking to replace your spouse. Assuming you marriage was wonderful in every way, it is unrealistic to think that you will find someone who will fulfill you the way your late spouse did. Of course, if you wanted to kill him had he not died without your help, it doesn't matter. What you are looking for is not a replacement but someone who you can share your life with.

- ***There are no rules as to how long you should grieve after the loss of a spouse***

  In our grandparents' generation, there were unofficial but often followed set periods of mourning. Anyone who has been married already comes with memories of a previous relationship. These may be loving and happy ones, or in some cases they may be painful or bitter. So it is important to know that you have given yourself time to grieve over your loss.

- ***Do not remarry because of outside influences or worry about what others may think***

  Friends and family may urge you to look for another partner. Or, once you start dating, you may become a target of public opinion that you have not grieved long enough. The decision to remarry is yours alone. Besides, why should you deprive yourself at a second chance of happiness?

LEGALLY SPEAKING! Sadly, "until death do us part" terminates the marriage contract. Though a person who has lost a spouse is referred to as a widow or widower, as the marriage contract no longer exists, your legal status is single.

See Chapter Chapter Twenty-Five for a discussion of marrying a widower (er)

LISTEN TO THE VOICES OF PUBLIC OPINION

Y ou met the person of your dreams. She is so beautiful. He is amazing. The wedding date is set and the invitations are in the mail. Finally, the big day arrives. As you walk down the aisle, you view a sea of smiles. Out of the corner of your eye, you also see some smirks lurking within the smiles? And are you crazy but do you also sense that some of your guests are murmuring something amongst themselves?

Fortunately, as you continue the walk and approach the altar, music deafens all other sounds, and in a few moments you are pronounced husband and wife and live happily ever after. STOP. Perhaps you should have listened to the voices of public opinion before you said I do as behind those smiles may have been warnings given to you before that memorable day. But you were too much in love to read all those messages. The ones you did read you paid little attention to. In looking back, you probably wished that you had taken the time to read rather than speed.

Too often in our rush to get married, we forget about or choose not to listen to our family and friends. Of course the ultimate decision as to whom you marry is yours alone. But sometimes, our judgments get clouded by the excitement of getting married and we fail to listen to public opinion. Before you walk, open you ears, and listen. Don't hold an election and forget to count the ballots. Read the signs that pop up along the road to remarriage.

♛ EVERYBODY'S TALKING BUT YOU'RE NOT LISTENING

Don't you hate it when someone says, "I told you so." It forces you to admit you were wrong and no one likes to do that. If you look back at the critics who were not writing raving reviews of the man or woman you were supposedly about to spend the rest of your life with, they told you so, and had you listened to them then you would not be reading this book now.

Before trying to get it right the second time around, pay special attention to the people in your life who sincerely have your best interest at heart.

PRACTICAL POINT: When given advice, always consider the source. Is this person sincerely looking out for my best interests or simply jealous of me?

KERRI'S STORY

Kerri divorced her first husband Steve after learning he had several affairs during their marriage. Prior to walking down the aisle, her father told her that "he knew guys like Steve and warned her that he was a player." She ignored her Dad's advice which was also shared by her brother. Instead, she sided with her mother who thought Steve was very charming.

After only six months of being single again, she met Jack who was ten years older than her and had two divorces under his belt. Once again, Kerri's father warned her that this was not the type of man she should consider as a marriage partner. Once again, she was blinded by his charm only to find herself in our office a year later ending marriage number two! In Kerri's case, her "father does know best!"

♛ YOUR FRIENDS CAN'T ALL BE WRONG

When you are dating, it is sometimes easy to lose your objectivity. To you, he is amazing and wonderful. Why would you want to hear anything negative about him? But when the relationship turns to the possibility of marriage, it is time to listen to the voices of public opinion.

ALLISON'S STORY

Allison began dating Rick after graduating college. She said his best quality was that he made her laugh. Unfortunately, her best friends did not see the humor and found Rick to be a phony. But they kept their opinions to themselves rather than sharing them with Allison as they expected she would break up with Rick in due time.

To their surprise, after a year of dating, Allison announced that she was engaged. She was quite upset when her two best friends did not react with enthusiasm when they heard the news. In fact, they were brutally honest when they shared their opinions with her. Instead of listening, she chose to ignore their views concluding they were jealous of Allison meeting Mr. Right while they continued looking for that special person.

Only after her divorce was final did Allison admit to her two best friends they were right as they saw things in Rick that she was either ignoring or blind to.

Listen to your parents and friends and don't right away assume people are jealous or envious that you are getting remarried. If the source has always been sincere, there is no reason to doubt that person's sincerity now.

STEVE'S STORY

Steve was forty-two, never married when he met Rosanne. He was a software developer who licensed his programs to various companies. Financially, he had done very well but romantically he had not met the person to spend his life with. Rosanne had been married for less than a year. Steve met her online and admits that he was first attracted to her beauty as she had this "European seductive look." Together, they got along great. When she was introduced to his friends, the comments varied from, "She's a little rough around the edges" to "I wouldn't screw her with your dick." When their relationship became serious, his parents as well as his friends voiced their concerns. His mother described Rosanne as a "gold digger" out for her son's money. Despite all the public comment, Steve proceeded with wedding plans. Within six months, the European mystique began to wear off as Steve spent his time reading the credit card statements.

GETTING FINANCIALLY READY TO SAY
I DO AGAIN!

Unlike your first marriage where parents became financial partners and helped pay for the wedding, remarriages rarely include financial assistance from either side. Before you break your piggy bank, it is prudent advice to take inventory of your financial status.

♛ GET OUT OF DEBT!

We buy designer sunglasses, would prefer to stay at the Four Seasons rather than the Holiday Inn, and shop at Nordstrom instead of Wal-Mart. Why drive a Ford Taurus when the monthly payment on a new Beemer is only another $100 bucks a month. It's only a lease anyway! Besides, my neighbor drives a Beemer. Why drink Trader Joe's Two Buck Chuck when one of those credit cards in our wallet or purse will pay for a fine bottle of cabernet.

All the above is so true.(but) But here's the problem. Credit cards are only occupying space in your wallet. They are not paying your bills for you but are just a vehicle to extend your debt. The inability to pay your debts may only add unwanted and unneeded stress to a new marriage. Accordingly, before you say I do again, concentrate on eliminating or managing your bills.

LEGALLY SPEAKING! If you are having bill paying problems, you may wish to consult with Consumer Credit Counselors. They are a non-profit organization that helps people reorganize their debts. With offices nationwide, you can locate an office near you by going online or checking your phone book for a local listing. If your debts are no longer manageable and you have exhausted all available remedies to pay your bills, you may want to consult with a bankruptcy attorney to discuss discharging your bills or working out a repayment of your debts through a court approved plan. Note, in most cases, you are still able to keep your home and car.

♛ THE FIRST TIME AROUND WAS FOR LOVE— SECURING YOUR FINANCIAL FUTURE

If you are under thirty, you can probably skip this chapter as you will hopefully have many opportunities to meet your next Mr. or Mrs. Right, fall in love, and live happily ever after. But as we get older, we start to prioritize what is important in life. Partying till the sun rises is great unless you have kids that you need to make breakfast for that morning.

As a result, what starts to become important is not only who you are with today but what happens if you are alone tomorrow. To illustrate, you do not have to read a newspaper or research online to know that:

- It is becoming more and more difficult to afford a home.
- People who are forced to rent are unhappy as they would prefer to own where they live.
- Rents are increasing as are the costs of gasoline, food, utilities, and clothing.
- If you have to pay for medical insurance, you may need to get a second job.
- Our economy may be on the brink of another great depression!

With tax breaks that still benefit married couples, it is less expensive to be married than to be alone. That is not to say you should marry the first stray that walks past your table while sitting at Starbucks. In reality, you probably shouldn't be sitting in Starbucks paying $4.00 for a non-fat café latte.

Accordingly, evaluating your financial security must be part of your thought process before walking down the aisle the second time around.

JOLENE'S STORY

Jolene was thirty-five, divorced, and facing the prospect of being single for the rest of her life. She was renting a one bedroom apartment and wanted to move into something bigger but could not afford to pay more rent.

She met James, age forty, who was single, never married, and was also renting. James worked as a car salesman and was paid by commission. Unbeknownst to Jolene, he had a prior bankruptcy.

After a few weeks, Jolene and James were dating exclusively and after a few more months, they decided to move into together and were able to afford a two bedroom apartment on their combined incomes. To pay for their wedding reception, they charged and took cash advances against their credit cards. They also financed a new car, their bedroom furniture, and honeymoon. Within a year, James was laid off from his job as car sales were slow. He then went from dealership to dealership only working a few months at each new job only to be laid off again. Meanwhile, with all their debts in both their names, and with only Jolene working, it became impossible to pay their creditors.

As is typical for couples saddled with debt, their money problems consumed their marriage and soon ended in divorce. That of course did not stop the creditors who pursued Jolene as she was the only one working. She eventually filed for bankruptcy which destroyed her credit of which she had worked so hard to build up from the time she first started working.

Jolene's story illustrates what happens when you marry for love without giving enough thought to financial security. The fact that James had filed bankruptcy before should have been a warning to her that financial security could be tenuous if she married him. Of course, no one can predict whether our country will fall into a depression and suddenly we are all out of work.

However in choosing the person to remarry, you need to think beyond the wedding ceremony and ask:

• Would you be comfortable making a loan to this person confident that you would be paid back?

- Will this person give you the financial security you need and deserve?
- Can you trust this person to make prudent business decisions?
- Will this person communicate and not deceive or withhold information about your finances?

Remember, no one has a crystal ball to predict the future. It does not matter how much money you make or whether you are about to inherit from your parent's estate in the future as tomorrow you may be disabled! Ideally, you need to have a plan for today!

See Chapter Nineteen for a discussion of investigating your future spouse's credit before you say I do, again!

SPECIAL SITUATION—SOCIAL SECURITY BENEFITS

If you were receiving social security benefits based on your former husband's earnings, and now remarry, you will lose those benefits. However, you will become eligible to receive benefits from your current spouse's social security earnings provided you are married for at least twelve months.

JOAN'S STORY

Joan was married to Jim who was ten years older than her. When they divorced, he was already receiving social security. As a result, she was entitled to receive her share of his monthly benefits. When she remarried Aaron, he too was receiving social security. However, his monthly amount was less than what Jim received. As a result, Joan lost her monthly benefits through Jim's account. Furthermore, if Aaron and her divorced after twelve months, or Aaron passed away, her monthly benefits would be less than if she remained married to Jim.

For more information about Social Security benefits, contact the Social Security Administration at 1-800-772-1213 or check online at www.ssa.gov.

CHAPTER THIRTEEN

♔ FINANCIAL BENEFITS TO NOT REMARRYING

For some, remarriage may not always be a cure for securing your financial future. In fact, the United States Census Bureau has determined that over the past several years, the number of persons who choose to live together without benefit of marriage is growing at an accelerating pace. These people recognize that marriage has some drawbacks:

- If you are receiving alimony, (referred to in some states as spousal support) that amount will terminate upon your remarriage.
- Children from a previous marriage might be resentful of your new spouse, fearful that they might lose their inheritance.
- Persons who remarry may jeopardize their entitlements to certain types of retirement benefits that originated with their former spouse and terminate upon remarriage.
- If you file a joint return, regardless of whether one or both of you are working, you are both legally responsible for the payment of taxes. Therefore, if the remarriage fails, you could still owe Uncle Sam money for unpaid taxes.
- Depending on the income of your intended spouse, your own income might be taxed at a higher rate than if you had remained single.
- Your assets will be vulnerable in the event your new spouse requires expensive medical or long-term care, even if the assets remain in your name alone.

GETTING LEGALLY READY FOR REMARRIAGE

Before you are blinded by love, stop to consider all the other persons who are already in your life and may be dependent upon you. Then ask yourself the most unthinkable of questions. That is, what will happen to all these people if I am no longer here? How will they be provided for? How will they survive? Unless you have some form of Estate Planning in place, your loved ones may have little time to grieve as they will be scrambling to put together the pieces of the puzzle that your passing has now shattered.

☙ WILLS, TRUSTS, AND ESTATE PLANNING

When contemplating marriage for a second time, especially when you have children from a previous marriage, it is highly recommended that you complete some type of Estate planning before you walk down the aisle. This way, you assure that your children and any others you choose will share in your Estate. Otherwise, depending on your state law, your spouse may receive all of your assets despite any protests from your family.

LEGALLY SPEAKING! Though the Internet can provide excellent information about Estate Planning, it is always recommended that you speak directly with an attorney in deciding upon your Estate planning needs.

There are two types of documents that can provide for how you want your assets distributed upon your passing; Wills and Trusts.

♛ WHAT A WILL DOES

In simplest terms, a Will is your letter of instructions for the person you appoint as your Executor to carry out your last wishes when you are no longer here to speak for yourself.

Your wishes may describe how you want your property to be divided, including specific bequests naming the individuals to receive your property. Without such a document, your property will be distributed based on your state's law known as Intestate Succession.

However, that formula for distribution may be counter to what your wishes are. To illustrate, you may be estranged from your only child and wish that your entire estate go to your brother. However, without a Will, most states would distribute your assets to your son or daughter, regardless of what your relationship with him or her was.

In addition, you may express in your Will your wishes regarding final interment; that is burial or cremation.

SPECIAL SITUATION—DEATH OF CUSTODIAL PARENT AND YOUR CHOICE FOR GUARDIANSHIP

It is a common misnomer that upon the death of a parent who has custody, the noncustodial parent automatically gets custody of the children. Though in most cases this would be correct, if you have strong feelings about who should raise your children upon your passing, and you state your wishes in your Will, most courts will be willing to consider your appointment for guardian before placing custody with your Ex.

STACY'S STORY

Stacy was involved in a volatile marriage with Andy as he was abusive both verbally and physically toward her. On two occasions, Stacy called the police which led to Andy being convicted of domestic violence for which he had to attend anger management classes. Fortunately, he never hit the children. After their divorce, Stacy was diagnosed with terminal cervical cancer. Prior to her death, she made her Will in which she stated that she wanted her sister to raise her two children.

Upon her passing, Stacy's sister took temporary custody of the children though she granted Andy visitation. However, he wanted the kids to move in with him to which the sister refused citing Stacy's wishes.

Andy retained an attorney to seek custody. After a trial in which Andy's violent history was made known to the court, custody was awarded to the sister as the court took into consideration Stacy's will which expressed her desire in having her sister be the legal guardian.

❦ WHAT A TRUST DOES

A living trust is similar to a will in that it sets out how you wish to divide your property. The major difference is that it avoids probate which can be very expensive for the Estate. In a trust, you appoint someone to "step into your shoes," who can act on the behalf of the Estate without the requirement of court supervision after you are no longer here.

> LEGALLY SPEAKING! Regardless of whether you have a Will or not, if your estate value exceeds a certain monetary amount as set by your state law, before your property can be distributed to your beneficiaries that you have named, it must be probated. By making a trust, probate is often avoided.

❦ THE NOT SO OBVIOUS REASONS WHY YOU SHOULD HAVE SOME TYPE OF ESTATE PLANNING

The following two stories should help you consider whether you need Estate planning:

HE WOULD HAVE WANTED A TRADITIONAL BURIAL

Joel married Diane. It was the second marriage for both of them. Joel was Jewish, not very religious but enjoyed the traditions and customs. His children from his first marriage had Bar Mitzvahs, and Diane and Joel had a reform Rabbi preside over their wedding ceremony. Diane was not an observant. Though they always talked about putting something in writing, they did not have a Will or Trust.

Joel died tragically in an auto accident. His parents, when contacted by Diane, were told that she was going to have his body cremated. His parents voiced their objection saying it was the Jewish custom to bury and that Joel would have wanted it that way. Furthermore, because of Jewish law, it was required to have a burial immediately. Diane told them, that, as Joel's wife, she would decide and it was her final decision to cremate her husband.

As a result, Joel's parents went to an attorney to seek an injunction stopping any plans Diane had made for cremation until a judge ruled on the issue. After two weeks had passed, there was a court hearing. Despite Joel's parents' plea, the court found in favor of the wife in the absence of a Will that stated otherwise.

His Son Was Left Out On The Street!

Toby was introduced to Brian through a mutual friend. Brian was a widower and raising his fifteen-year-old son. Toby was divorced and had a daughter. When the two were married, they decided to move into Toby's home which she received in her divorce. Life was great but quickly turned upside down when Brian was diagnosed with a rare form of leukemia. He died after a three month battle just short of their three month wedding anniversary. His only asset was the $90,000 in his 401k retirement plan which was originally left to his first wife. But when he married Diane, he had never changed the name of the beneficiary. Under the laws of the state where Brian and Toby resided, a surviving spouse is entitled to the money held in a retirement account if a beneficiary is not named. When Brian's son graduated high school, having turned eighteen, Toby had no further legal responsibility for providing for him and promptly showed him the front door. What's more, she never shared with him any part of the $90,000.

♛ SCHEDULE A LEGAL CHECKUP

I see my doctor every year for an annual physical. Even if you are not having any problems, an annual checkup is a good preventative measure to take as something may be discovered which, if you had waited, could lead to more serious problems later on.

Likewise after a divorce, and before contemplating marriage for the second time, I highly recommend that you perform a self-examination of your legal affairs to make sure everything is in order. If something does not seem right or needs to be changed, now is the time to do it!

A legal checkup may require a review of the following:

✓ CHILD SUPPORT ORDERS

If you are a custodial parent receiving child support, you need to consult with an attorney to determine if the amount you receive will be affected by your remarriage. Specifically, you should ask if your new spouse's income will be considered by the court if your Ex should consider seeking a reduction of the amount you receive.

LEGALLY SPEAKING! Divorce laws vary from state to state as to whether a new spouse's income is viewed in determining the amount of support.

SPECIAL SITUATION: RELOCATON AFTER DIVORCE

What if your divorce agreement says you cannot relocate out of the state and your fiancé's job is being relocated out of state? By the terms of your divorce agreement, without prior court approval, you would be in contempt of court if you were to move.

BONNIE'S STORY

Bonnie was a divorced for five years when she started dating Joe. Joe was a sales manager for a large office supply company. During their courtship, Joe was offered a position as national sales manager. However, the job required that he move to Atlanta where the company was based.

Bonnie informed her Ex whom she had an amicable relationship with about her plans to move with Joe. When he heard the news, he became deeply upset. Their children were eight and ten, and the thought that his visitations would be reduced from every weekend to summer vacations was not acceptable. While Bonnie went ahead with her marriage plans, her former husband retained an attorney seeking a restraining order preventing Bonnie from leaving.

After an ugly, protracted hearing, the court did decide to amend the original court order deciding it should not interfere with a financial opportunity for Bonnie and her new husband which could eventually be in the best interest of the children.

Though the result was favorable to Bonnie, not all cases conclude this way. Accordingly, if you are faced with issues of relocation that may be counter to what is written in a divorce agreement, consult with an attorney.

✓ LAST WILL AND TESTAMENT

If you have made a Will while you were married, you probably left part or all of your estate to your Ex spouse. Depending on your state law, you may need to update or amend your Will. This is because the laws of inheritance vary from state to state. Not all states take the position that simply because you are divorced, your Ex loses his inheritance rights. Instead, your state may still enforce the right of your former spouse named in your Will to inherit your Estate.

LEGALLY SPEAKING! Many states have adopted what is known as the Uniform Probate Code. In such cases, if someone dies without a will, any property would automatically be inherited according to bloodline. Therefore, if you were married but now divorced, and are survived by your Ex husband and your parents, your parents and not your Ex would inherit your estate.

✓ GUARDIANSHIPS

If you have children and made a Will during marriage, the document most likely included a guardianship clause in which you named a primary as well as an alternate person to care and raise your child if you and your spouse passed away.

Now that you are divorced, you may wish to revisit this document to update it. For example, during your marriage, you may have named your in-laws to raise your children if you and your spouse were someday not here. However, your feelings for your in-laws may now have changed. Unless you also physically change your Will, what is stated in that document will be enforceable as your last wishes.

✓ LIVING TRUSTS

If you and your former spouse had made a trust, the assets that were originally placed in it have probably now been redistributed to each of you as your separate property. That is because the court, or you and your spouse through a property settlement agreement, divided your assets. As such, it may be your intentions to maintain the identify of this property as your separate property. Accordingly, you should consult with an attorney about making a new trust in your name alone and transfer those assets into your trust. By doing so, the trust would contain language that sets out how you wish for your assets(to) be distributed upon your passing.

LEGALLY SPEAKING! There are many types of trusts but the most common is known as a Revocable Living Trust. By creating this document, you control the assets during your lifetime. However, upon your passing, you name someone to "step into your shoes" to carry out your wishes as if you were here. This person is known as your successor trustee.

✓POWERS OF ATTORNEY

There are two common powers of attorney; a power of attorney to make health decisions and a power of attorney to make financial decisions. Both powers allow you to appoint someone to make health and financial decisions for you in the event you become physically incapacitated or mentally incompetent to make decisions for yourself.

Typically, when married one spouse appoints the other to make these decisions. However, unless these documents have been updated, your Ex would still have the power to act despite the fact you are now divorced!

SAM'S STORY

During their marriage, Sam and Susan had reciprocal powers of attorney wherein they appointed each other to make financial decisions if one of them could not. Shortly after they divorced, Sam was diagnosed with an aggressive stomach cancer.

One of the assets of the marriage was a rental property which the parties had agreed to hold onto and not sell until the market improved. However, Susan, without Sam's knowledge, listed the property for sale and provided her agent a copy of the power of attorney which gave her the authority to make financial decisions for Sam.

Sam died never knowing what Susan had done. But his children from his first marriage found out what she had done and filed an action against her to recover their Dad's share of the proceeds from the sale of the property.

SPECIAL SITUATION: REMARRIAGE LATER IN LIFE

Finding love later in life may be unexpected and exciting, but should it lead to marriage? The considerations are much different for an older couple with adult children and retirement plans than for a young couple just starting out. Before deciding whether to get married or just live together, you need to look at your estate plan, Social Security benefits, and potential long-term care needs, among other things. Whatever you decide to do, you may want to consult a lawyer to make sure your wishes will be carried out.

Here are some issues to consider:

- **Estate Planning**

Getting married can have a big effect on your estate plan. Even if you don't include a new spouse in your will, in most states spouses are automatically entitled to a share of your estate (usually one-third to one-half). One way to prevent a spouse from taking his or her share is to enter into a prenuptial agreement in which both spouses agree not to take anything from the other's estate. If you want to leave something to your spouse and ensure your heirs receive their inheritance, a trust may be the best option.

- **The Family Home**

If the residence is in your name, before combining households you will need to think about what will happen to the house once you die. If you want to keep the house within your family, putting the house in both spouse's names is not an option. On the other hand, you may not want your heirs to evict your surviving spouse upon your passing. One solution is for you to give your surviving spouse a life estate. Once the surviving spouse dies, the house will pass to your heirs.

- **Social Security**

Many divorced or widowed seniors receive Social Security from their former spouses, and remarriage can affect benefits. If you are a widow(er) or divorced and you remarry before age sixty, you will not be able to receive Social Security retirement benefits based on your deceased or divorced spouse's work record. You will still receive benefits, however, as long as you remarry after age sixty. You may also be able to collect spousal benefits from a new spouse if those benefits are higher.

- **Alimony**

If you are receiving alimony from a divorced spouse, it will likely end once you remarry. Depending on the laws in your state and divorce settlement, alimony may end even if you simply live with someone else.

- **Survivor's Annuities**

Widows and widowers of public employees, such as police officers and firefighters, often receive survivor's annuities. Many of these annuities end if the surviving spouse remarries. In addition, widows and widowers of military personnel may lose their annuities if they remarry before age fifty-seven. Before getting married, check your annuity policy to see what the effect will be.

- ***College Financial Aid***
  Single parents with children in college may want to reconsider before getting married. A new spouse's income could affect the amount of financial aid the college student receives. Some private colleges may even count the combined income of a couple who lives together if they commingle their expenses.

SPECIAL SITUATION—YOU'RE STILL MARRIED!!!

In a perfect world, only people who are single get married. Since there are laws that prohibit being married to more than one person at the same time, a marriage license cannot be issued if you state you are still married.

What if you do not know whether your divorce is final? Note, the County Clerk accepts what you have stated on your marriage application as the truth as you are signing it "under penalty of perjury." Moreover, clerks do not have the resources to research whether the information that you have provided is correct. For this reason, before you say I do, again, make sure you are divorced. Otherwise, if you later find out that your first marriage was not terminated by the court, your second marriage will not be valid.

♛ NUNC PRO TUNC DIVORCE

The invitations are in the mail and then you get the shock of your life. You are still married. After some quick investigation on your part, you find out that your Ex who was supposed to complete the paperwork dropped the ball. What do you do? Fortunately, the courts have a solution as this is a more common problem than you might think. In such situations, upon a proper showing of cause, like I am getting married tomorrow, you can apply to the court for what is known as a Nunc Pro Tunc Divorce, which is a Latin phrase and fancy way of saying, "Please back date my divorce so that I can get married."

LEGALLY SPEAKING! HBO's popular show Big Love is about plural marriages where a husband has several wives. The legal term for multiple marriages at the same time is bigamy and such an act is a crime in all fifty states. Therefore, before proceeding down the aisle the second time, make sure that your and (if applicable) your fiancé's prior marriage has been dissolved.

SPECIAL SITUATION—YOU ARE STILL MARRIED IN THE EYES OF YOUR FAITH

Even though the judge has pronounced you are once again a single person, he is sitting on a bench in a civil courtroom. However, your religious beliefs may require that you seek a divorce from a higher source.

✿ THE JEWISH GET

A Get is a religious document that separates the combined soul of the man and woman. It makes no reference to fault and has no bearing on any property settlement agreement or court order signed by a Judge in a civil court.

Without a proper Get, even though the man and woman have physically separated, they are still bound together metaphysically and considered as if fully married. This is true to the extent that if the woman were to have relations with another man before receiving a Get, it would be considered as adultery.

A secular or divorce does not count for a Get as it must be written in a very specific way, and can be done so only by someone who is well-versed in Jewish law (i.e. not "just any rabbi"). For example, the Get must be written specifically for this couple, and a pre-printed document cannot be used. There are also specific formulas for the spelling of words and names. There are other factors as well, including the type of people who must witness the giving of the Get and all these factors must be done properly, or else the couple is still considered as fully married.

PRACTICAL POINT! If you have strong religious convictions, getting a Get solves a lot of problems down the line. To illustrate, if you were divorced for many years and now want to remarry, you need a Get. But if you didn't take care of it at the time you were divorced, and your Ex has moved, it may be difficult to locate him. Furthermore, after all this time, he may not be as willing to cooperate with you.

✿ THE CATHOLIC ANNULMENT PROCESS

The Catholic Church teaches that, even after a divorce, a valid marriage remains in force unless and until it is proven otherwise. Therefore, no one who has been previously married can enter into a Catholic marriage until an annulment is granted. This is true whether the person is Catholic or not.

When a marriage ends in divorce, the Church provides both parties to that marriage with the right to petition the Church to determine whether or not a permanent marriage bond was created when the two parties entered into their marriage.

By granting an annulment, it is a statement by the Church that the enduring bond of a sacramental marriage was not present at the time of the marriage. This reality could be true for a number of different reasons that are unique to each marriage. Examples of these are immaturity or psychological factors that impeded the freedom of the parties entering into the marriage.

The annulment procedure includes questioning of family members, friends or counselors, who can provide testimony regarding the breakdown of the marriage.

Ch 15

Prenuptial and Postnuptial Agreements

T he previous chapter discusses the importance of a legal checkup prior to remarriage. Before you jump to the conclusion that as an attorney I just want to drum up business for my colleagues, consider the following:

If you were first married in your twenties, as a guy your most important assets were probably your old Junker car and a set of shot glasses. If you are female, chances are your most valued possessions were the set of dishes your Mom bought you from Pottery Barn or your closet full of jeans and tops that you are now embarrassed to admit you ever wore.

Now that you are older and wiser, hopefully your income has allowed you to buy a home, contribute to a retirement plan, and make some prudent investments. You may have also started your own business which, through your efforts will continue to prosper.

There is also someone special in your life as you have met the person of your dreams. Of course that is what you said about your Ex, but this person is different. He or she loves you for who you are. She is not materialistic. He works and doesn't need your money. Together you can now go off and live forever in marriage heaven. WRONG! Before you go shopping for the ring or picking out a dress, you need to legally protect your hard earned assets acquired before remarriage.

✿ PRENUPTIAL AGREEMENTS 101—A QUICK LESSON

A Prenuptial Agreement, also known as a Premarital Agreement in some states, is a contract entered into between two parties before marriage. The purpose of the agreement is to define for the couple what the disposition of their financial assets will be in the event of divorce or death. Additionally, a prenuptial agreement allows you to supersede state laws that dictate how your estate should be distributed.

A properly drafted agreement will accomplish the following:

- It will identify each party's property that was acquired before marriage
- It will protect and insulate yourself from debts that the other party had before marriage and incurred during marriage
- It will set out the amount of support one spouse may have to pay to the other and the duration of time that support will be payable if the parties subsequently divorce
- It will provide for compensation to one spouse upon divorce if she had to give up a high paying job and relocate for the sake of the marriage

In order to be valid, a prenuptial agreement must be signed by both parties prior to the wedding. The agreement will ordinarily be enforced if it is executed properly which means that, depending on your state law, the document may have to be witnessed by two or more persons, notarized, or both. In addition, to be valid, the parties must have entered into the contract freely as any evidence of fraud or duress involved in its execution will make the contract void.

Note, if you do not have a prenuptial agreement the laws of divorce of the state you reside in at the time of your divorce will apply and the laws of inheritance will apply if you die.

✿ WHAT ARE THE LAWS OF INHERITANCE?

The laws of inheritance vary from state to state. In some states, a surviving spouse may inherit all of your property. This may create a problem if you have children from a previous marriage. In other states the spouse may be entitled to a percentage of your Estate even if there are surviving children.

WHAT ARE THE LAWS OF DIVORCE?

These laws are also complicated and vary greatly depending if your state follows community property law or is a noncommunity property state. As a general rule, the courts have a great deal of discretion in awarding alimony and dividing property.

In addition, the longer you are married, the more likely it is that your entire estate will be divided equally with your spouse upon divorce. In a short-term marriage, the most typical approach is to return the parties to the situation they were in before they got married.

However, there is no hard and fast rule on what constitutes a short-term marriage or a long-term one. The courts can consider as factors what your assets were at the time of the marriage, but merely because they were assets acquired before the marriage does not exempt them from division at the time of divorce.

If there are any extenuating circumstances a court can award alimony or divide assets to aid a sick or disabled spouse even if the marriage was for a very short period of time. Courts are also entitled to consider marital fault when dividing assets and awarding alimony so there is no way of completely anticipating what will happen to your property in the event of divorce.

SO WHY HAVE A PRENUPTIAL AGREEMENT IF STATE LAWS COVER THESE THINGS?

The reason to have a prenuptial agreement is that you can try to determine in advance how to handle inheritance and division of assets and alimony on divorce. If you desire a greater degree of certainty you can expect that under most circumstances a judge will enforce a validly executed prenuptial agreement. For example, if it is your view that you want all of your premarital property to remain yours in the event of divorce, and go to your parents, or children from a prior marriage, upon your death, that is something that will likely be enforced in a prenuptial agreement, but without a prenuptial agreement state law would generally not permit.

With respect to alimony, the case law is a little less clear. But if a prenuptial agreement contains a provision in which both parties waive alimony, this provision will generally be enforced, at least in a short-term marriage.

LEGALLY SPEAKING! Though it is an agreement between the parties, some states look at such documents as against "public policy" and may hold certain sections unenforceable. For example, in California, the courts have ruled that it is unfair for a spouse in advance of marriage, to waive any right to receive support if the marriage fails. In such cases, a prenuptial agreement with such a clause would not hold up in a divorce proceeding. Accordingly, before drafting your own agreement, it is advisable to have the document prepared by an attorney who specializes in family law.

❦ THE UNROMANTIC SIDE OF PRENUPTIAL AGREEMENTS

While deciding on invitations, whom to invite to the wedding, and where to honeymoon, sitting down with your fiancé and having him put his John Hancock on a prenuptial agreement is far from being romantic. However, statistics do not favor second marriages. You should not let love get in the way of protecting your future and holding on to what you may have worked hard to acquire.

On the other hand, asking your intended to enter into a premarital agreement raises the presumption that the marriage may not work out. That is true because it goes against the idea that marriage is forever. Likewise, marriage is a partnership. Sometimes, despite the best intentions, partners disagree and then go their separate ways. The purpose of a prenuptial agreement is to insure that whatever you bring into the partnership leaves with you when you leave.

Regardless, such documents are often looked upon by the person with fewer assets as a threat to the marriage. Furthermore, it is common for one party to have more assets than the other and therefore has more of a need to protect those assets. As a result, there is no easy and reassuring way to explain to the spouse without assets your intentions except to say that the document is necessary only as a preventive measure and hopefully will never be needed. Relaying to your intended spouse the following two stories will also help illustrate how important the document can be.

DAD DIES AND BOYS GET NOTHING!

Craig was married before and had two children who were now teenagers. He met Cynthia who had never been married and was ten years younger than he was. Craig published magazines catering to boat owners which were very profitable. Craig and Cynthia married. However, two years later he was diagnosed with inoperable colon cancer. Despite aggressive treatment, Craig died. On behalf of the boys, Craig's Ex-wife filed a probate action to have the business asset declared an asset of her sons. The court however ruled in favor of Cynthia. As a result, under that state's law which gave everything to a surviving spouse, Craig's sons received nothing!

COURT SPLITS DAUGHTER'S INHERITANCE

Jeannie's mother died leaving her a coin collection which her mother had inherited from her father. When Jeannie married Mitch, they had the collection appraised and the estimated value ranged from $100,000 to $150,000. Mitch had a gambling problem and could not hold onto a job. After five years, Jenanie called its quits and filed for divorce. To her surprise, Mitch claimed an interest in the coin collection that was now worth over $200,000. Because Jeannie had no proof of when she acquired the collection (her Mom did not leave a Will) the court decided that the coin collection was community property and ordered that it be sold and the profits divided.

When couples consider prenuptial agreements, what often comes to mind are stories where one spouse walks away with nothing from the marriage despite her efforts of caring for the children. This is because of some piece of paper she signed before the marriage as to what she would be entitled to if the marriage failed. The two examples, above, demonstrate how unfair it would be if courts had to decide the distribution of property which might be in total contradiction of what was the intent of loved ones who left property or to spouses who died not being able to provide for their children.

LEGALLY SPEAKING! In most states, assets acquired during the marriage are considered property of the marriage. That is, if you later divorce, each party may make a claim to that property. Additionally, income that you earned during marriage is viewed as individual property.

However, if you live in Arizona, California, Idaho, Louisiana, Nevada, New Mexico, Texas or Washington, which are community property states, property acquired before marriage or during marriage by inheritance is deemed separate property. As a result, in a divorce, your spouse would not be entitled to any share of that property. However, unless that property is clearly identified as separate property at the inception of the marriage, it may become difficult to prove its identify if you should later divorce. As a result, so that there is no question as to what is yours and what is his, many couples enter into prenuptial agreement before you say I do, again.

♛ DO I NEED A PRENUPTIAL AGREEMENT?

Most of my colleagues take the position that everyone who enters into a marriage with property of value acquired before the marriage should have a prenuptial agreement. The truth is, however, most people do not have such agreements. Probably the most common reason why people steer away from signing is because the concept of a prenuptial agreement runs counter to the idea of marriage; that is you are marrying someone you love but at the same time negotiating the terms of the divorce settlement.

♛ A CHECKLIST FOR WHEN A PRENUPTIAL AGREEMENT SHOULD BE CONSIDERED:

If one or more of the spouses:
- ✓ owns real property
- ✓ owns or has an interest in a business or is owed money from the sale of a business
- ✓ owns personal property that has more than negligible value
- ✓ has children from a previous marriage
- ✓ is named as a beneficiary in someone's Will or Trust

A sample prenuptial agreement is found in Appendix A.

PRACTICAL POINT! Often cited as one of the most important qualities a person looks for in a future spouse is trust. Logically, if you approach the subject of a prenuptial agreement and the response is an absolute NO without consideration, proceed cautiously. You may think you know this person you are about to marry but maybe you DON'T.

♛ ALTERNATIVES TO PRENUPTS

If the idea of a prenuptial agreement is so distasteful, I suggest the following:
- Each party should make a list of all of his or her property that was acquired before marriage. You may want to have the other party sign or initial the list.

- During the marriage, continue to treat any separate property as yours and not ours. That is, if you have a bank account that was created before marriage, do not put money into that account that was acquired during marriage. Therefore, if the marriage fails, you will be able to trace the identity of the account by proving that no marital property was deposited during marriage. This will assure that the court will find the account was yours before marriage.

- Do not change the identity of separate property. Legally, when separate property changes identity, it is known as "transmutation," which is an ugly sounding word but basically means it has lost its legal identity as separate property. By setting out your assets in a prenuptial agreement, and having the other side acknowledge these assets are yours, he cannot later challenge the identity of the asset and claim an interest in those assets in a subsequent divorce proceeding.

♛ WHEN TO HAVE THE TALK?

A prenuptial agreement should be drawn up at least two to three months before your wedding to avoid either party later claiming that he signed the document under duress. In addition, I highly recommend that the agreement be prepared by an attorney who represents you. In order to avoid any conflict of interest, your fiancé should have the agreement reviewed by his attorney before he signs it.

PRACTICAL POINT! Bringing up the subject of prenuptial agreements with your fiancé should not be something you fear. Sure it is easier to ask him what movie he wants to see or where he wants to go eat. But having a frank and honest relationship before you say I do again will often lead to open communication during the marriage.

♛ SPECIAL SITUATION: OOPS—YOU ARE ALREADY REMARRIED: POSTNUPTIAL AGREEMENTS

If you have already remarried, you may wish to consult with a family law attorney to create a postnuptial agreement. This document works the same way as a prenuptial agreement and protects your assets acquired before marriage. However, depending on the length of your remarriage, there may be other issues that did not exist before you said I do, again.

Are You Ready for Remarriage?

Are you ready for remarriage? Part Two of this book discusses what you need to do before you say I do, again. This includes having an emotional, financial, and legal checkup. So, if you think you are there, ask yourself the following questions. For each question, the desired response is whether you strongly agree. Note, there is no score and you are the grader. After taking the test you discover there are still areas that you cannot answer with confidence, you are not ready to say I do, again.

❦ PRIOR MARRIAGE

- I no longer hold any anger or resentment toward my Ex.
- Thoughts of my first marriage are no longer part of my daily life.
- Regardless of who was at fault, I accept that my first marriage failed.
- When thinking about remarriage, I am not being unduly influenced by anyone including my fiancé, parents, or friends.
- (If applicable) If my Ex has already remarried, I am not seeking re-marriage as a way to "get even".
- My Ex is not involved in my daily life.

I have been divorced at least two years or I feel a sufficient period of time has now passed and I have separated myself from married life and made the transition to single life.

❦ FINANCIAL WELL BEING

- I make my own financial decisions.
- I have established credit in my own name.
- I have little or no debt or have organized a plan to pay off my bills without being dependent upon family or friend support.
- I am saving or starting to save money for my future.
- I have updated any life insurance policies and, where applicable, removed my Ex's name as the beneficiary.
- When thinking about remarriage, I am not looking for someone to financially "bail me out".

❦ EMOTIONAL WELL BEING

- I am not addicted to alcohol or drugs.
- I am not in a treatment program for alcohol or drugs.
- I do not have any anger issues toward my Ex.
- I am not depressed and look forward to making a new life with my fiancé.
- I have surrounded myself with people who support me in a positive way.

❦ LEGAL WELL BEING

- I have updated any Wills, Trusts, and Powers of Attorney and, where applicable, removed my Ex's name.
- I have resolved all remaining issues of property division with my Ex.
- If applicable, I have resolved all issues regarding child support, custody, and visitation with my Ex.
- If I am the custodial parent, I am able to care for my children without the ongoing assistance of my Ex.
- When thinking about remarriage, I am not looking for a financial partner in raising my children.

CHAPTER SIXTEEN

♛ EMBRACING BEING SINGLE

- I have been living alone, with my children without a spousal substitute for two years or longer, or long enough to feel secure that I can live on my own again.
- I can take care of myself and do not need someone to do so.
- I have found confidence in reclaiming my single status.
- When thinking about remarriage, I am not seeking someone to change my life from misery to happiness.

♛ ABOUT REMARRIAGE

- I am not looking to remarry just because I want the title of a married person.
- I do not obsess about the day when I will walk down the aisle again.
- I have definite ideas about what my future spouse should be like.
- I will not settle for the sake of remarriage.

♛ (IF APPLICABLE) ABOUT YOUR FIANCÉ

I have met someone and have been in a serious relationship with this person for at least two years or long enough to know this person. Specifically, I am satisfied with what I know about:

- ✓ His health
- ✓ His finances
- ✓ His parents, siblings, and friends
- ✓ His values, goals, and ethics
- ✓ His views toward children

- I am in love with this person.
- I do not feel any pressure to marry this person but want to marry him.
- I accept this person and do not need to change him.

My Ten Step Quick Guide to Getting Ready to Say I Do, Again!

If you have bought any electronic device in the last ten years, it comes with a large operations manual as well as a quickstart guide. If you are anything like me and don't want to get bogged down with reading, you go for the quick guide. Accordingly, the following is my "Ten Step Quick Guide" to Getting Ready to Say I Do, again.

1. Resolve your first divorce

Before you seriously give any thought to remarriage, make sure you are emotionally, financially, and legally divorced from your first marriage.

2. Understand the mistakes you made the first time around

The simplest way of avoiding making the same mistakes again is by identifying what you may have done wrong in your first marriage.

3. Know everything there is to know about the person you are about to say I do to

Don't buy the box just because you like the outside wrapping. Get to really know your partner. Ask the difficult questions.

4. Be open and honest

Express your concerns and fears
Do not hold back.
Remarriages succeed when there is no fear of communication.

5. Consider marital counseling

Professional premarriage counseling may touch on issues that are difficult for you to address.

6. Get a fresh start

If that means moving, do so.

Evaluate who your true friends are and chuck those who do not have your best interests at heart.

Remember, you do not want any ghosts from your past to jeopardize your remarriage.

7. Embrace change

The first marriage is over and you should be open to trying new things and making adjustments that life may require.

Do not hang on to old habits that may have been irritating to your Ex.

8. Take inventory of your finances

Deal with money issues before you say I do, again. This may include seeking the advice of a financial planner.

9. Think Positive

Do not focus on the past but only the future.

10. Savor the moment

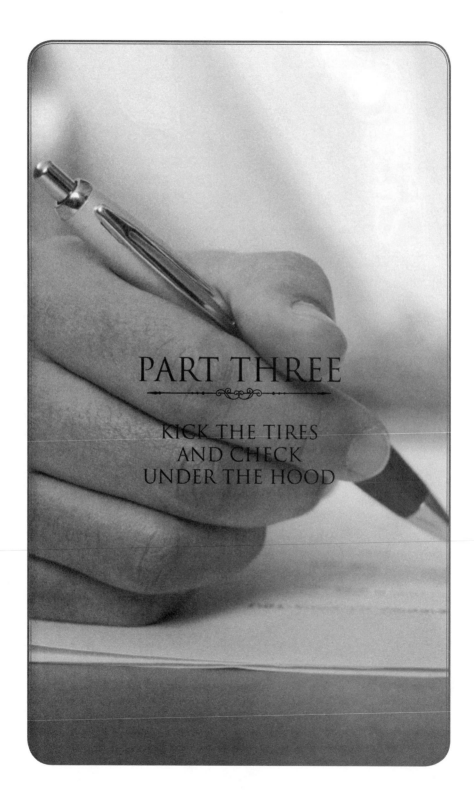

PART THREE

KICK THE TIRES
AND CHECK
UNDER THE HOOD

BUYER BEWARE!

Regardless of whether you are emotionally, financially, and legally ready to say I do, again, before you blissfully walk down the aisle you will want to make sure your bethrothed is also in good working order.

In its simplest form, finding the next person and the right person to spend the rest of your life with is similar to buying a used car. Unless you buy from a dealership, chances are the car you purchase does not come with a warranty. Accordingly, you will want to check the engine, kick the tires, take a test ride, and review the prior maintenance records of the vehicle before you write a check. You do this, because if something goes wrong, you're stuck with a lemon. Likewise, there is a no return policy on spouses. It is strictly "buyers beware." You would be wise to do your homework before signing on the dotted line.

> LEGALLY SPEAKING! There is a misnomer that if you buy a car and change your mind, there is a so called "cooling off period" wherein you can return it within three days. This is simply not true. Likewise, if after the honeymoon, you realize you got a lemon, you must file for divorce unless you qualify for an annulment which has very specific requirements.

♛ WHAT YOU DIDN'T DO THE FIRST TIME

In your excitement to get married the first time around you may have:

- ignored the voices of public opinion
- succumbed to family pressure to say I do
- did not ask questions about his physical and mental health
- did not do or complete a background check on your intended
- been blinded by love
- were fooled, lied to, or misrepresented as to who he was
- were in a coma, woke up on your wedding day, and went ahead with the wedding anyway!

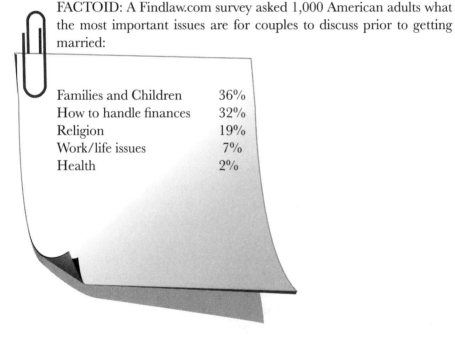

FACTOID: A Findlaw.com survey asked 1,000 American adults what the most important issues are for couples to discuss prior to getting married:

Families and Children	36%
How to handle finances	32%
Religion	19%
Work/life issues	7%
Health	2%

✿ MEDICAL HISTORY—A LOOK INTO THE PAST MAY BE A WINDOW INTO THE FUTURE

DISCLAIMER: Some readers may get quite upset after reading the next section as it could appear that I am placing a condition of health on remarriage. That is, whether your future spouse passes your medical evaluation should determine whether you should get married. You may also view my opinion as being inconsiderate and insensitive to persons with health issues. But going into a second marriage includes a higher risk of failure than the first time around. Therefore, while you should marry for love, it is also better to make an informed decision about your fiancé's heath issues before you say I do, again.

We are a society that is impressed with what is new. We want the latest cell phone that receives E-mail and the computer with lightning fast speed. We are also attracted to the now and wow restaurant that just opened up downtown. Likewise, when shopping for a car, do you want the shiny coupe with all the bells and whistles or the clunker with the trunk that does not close?

While it might sound cruel to compare finding your future spouse with shopping for a car, marriage under the best circumstances requires a lot of work to succeed. Marrying someone who has health issues may add further strain to the success of your marriage.

✿ A PHYSICAL CHECKLIST FOR LOVE

Before you say I do, again, you should have a serious discussion with your fiancé about his physical health. Ask him the following questions. You should also be prepared to share your health information.

✓ Do you have an annual physical examination?
✓ Do you take any prescribed or over-the-counter medications?
✓ Have you been diagnosed with any physical condition?
✓ Have you had any surgeries in the past five years?
✓ Have you had any outpatient hospital procedures done in the last five years?
✓ Did you ever smoke?
✓ Did you ever do illicit drugs?
✓ Have you ever been treated for a sexually transmitted disease?

✓ Are your parents/siblings alive? If not, what was the cause of their death?
✓ Does your family have any health issues?
✓ Does you family have any health issues that may be inherited?

STACY'S STORY

Stacy fell head over heels for John. He had never been married before and she had two children. Within a year they were tying the knot. Unfortunately, John did not disclose to his wife that he carried the gene for Marfan syndrome, an almost always fatal disease that he inherited from his father. Two years after marriage, John developed problems with breathing and was diagnosed with the same disease. He succumbed five years later.

Learning about one's health should not by itself be a reason not to walk down the aisle. But it is a window into what might be your future spouse's health issues. And, just like if you were buying a used car, you want to educate yourself about everything so that you can make an informed decision before you say I do, again!

PRACTICAL POINT! A congenital problem may also raise concerns if you and your fiancé are considering having children. If so, you may want to consult with a doctor for genetic testing.

CLAIRE'S STORY

Joel was thirty-seven and never married when he met Claire. She had been divorced for two years and was raising her teenage daughters. Joel admitted to having had numerous sexual partners but Claire was too embarrassed to ask him to be tested.

Within a year they were married and life was great until Claire had baby who was born with Herpes. She was outraged. She went to her doctor and suggested that she be tested for sexually transmitted diseases. Claire tested positive for Herpes 2 and her doctor said she could only contract it from sexual contact.

After confronting her husband about it, he admitted not telling her that he had the disease because he had not experiencd an outbreak for many years and "thought it was in remission."

LEGALLY SPEAKING! It is grounds for annulment if one spouse fails to disclose to the other something material about themselves prior to marriage. For example, if a spouse knows he cannot have children and does not reveal this to his future wife knowing she wants to start a family, most states would view this as a sufficient reason to annul the marriage.

♛ A MENTAL CHECKLIST FOR LOVE

Going to your doctor for an annual checkup will tell you if there is anything physically wrong. But if someone is having mental issues, such problems are not as easy to diagnose and just as easy to conceal. Accordingly, before you head to the altar, it is equally important to inquire about your fiancé's mental state of mind.

- ✓ Have you ever been addicted to drugs or alcohol or been diagnosed with any other addictive behavior?
- ✓ Have you ever been hospitalized or received medical care for a mental condition?
- ✓ Is there a history of mental illness in your family?
- ✓ Have you ever enrolled in an anger management class?
- ✓ Do you have any anger issues?
- ✓ Why did your prior marriage end?
- ✓ Have you ever been arrested for domestic violence or any related crime?

♛ RECOGNIZING THE WARNING SIGNS OF MENTAL INSTABILITY

When you approach a traffic signal, a yellow light means proceed with caution. If you are in a relationship with a person who exhibits signs of mental instability, think of it as a yellow light signal and proceed with the utmost care before heading down the road to the altar.

Accordingly, if you observe any of the following, it is time to pause and reassess:

He/she:
- has severe mood swings
- is verbally abusive
- becomes easily agitated
- has no social life outside of you

- is distrustful/suspicious of others where it is not warranted
- cannot hold down a job
- has a negative and pessimistic outlook on life

HOW SAD BUT TRUE! Upon reading this list you might ask yourself, "Who would ever stay with a person who behaved in such a manner. After giving it some thought, undoubtedly the name of some friend or family member who has stayed in such a relationship will come to mind.

PRACTICAL POINT! It is often difficult to have a conversation with someone that involves sensitive issues. It is better to find out now before you make a commitment. Most important, if you have any doubt, go with your gut feeling. If you think something is not right, it probably isn't. Remember it is your future you are deciding on. The consequences are small before you say I do than after!

Regardless, if you fear for your own safety, do not stay in the relationship out of fear. Likewise, feeling sorry for this person for what might happen if you leave is a terrible reason to stay.

SEX AND REMARRIAGE

On the divorce Richter scale, sex is rarely mentioned as a reason for the breakdown of a marriage. In fact, it seems that no matter how bad the marriage was, the sex was still good. Many of our clients reported having sex with their Ex even after the divorce was finalized. Perhaps sex was looked upon as a parting gift to each other for all of the years of pain.

Regardless, before you say I do again, you absolutely want to make sure that your partner operates well in the bedroom as well as in the rest of the house.

♛ HOUSTON, WE HAVE A PROBLEM!

Whether your fiancé can perform in the bedroom is not something that is usually revealed over an intimate dinner or by interviewing his friends. And with the introduction of the little blue pill, looks can be deceiving.

Therefore, unless for religious reasons, if you still consider yourself a virgin despite the fact that you were married before, you should test out the equipment before you buy. Once is not enough; just because the engine starts the first time, doesn't guarantee it will fire up again. Remember, marriage does not come with a warranty; it is strictly "buyer beware!"

MARK AND SHEILA'S STORY

Mark and Sheila were married before and both marriages ended bitterly. Other than a few disaster dates, Mark and Sheila were not in the dating game until they were introduced to each other by a friend. From their first date, Mark and Sheila realized they had a lot in common; they were both going to celebrate celebrating their 50th birthdays soon, they loved to travel, enjoyed the same foods, and shared a similar taste for music.

After three months Mark asked Sheila to go away with him for the weekend. Up until that point, they hadn't had sex but Sheila thought for sure this was the weekend it was going to happen. But by Sunday night, though they shared a bed together, nothing happened. Because she was of the generation where women were not supposed to be forward or be the aggressor, she said nothing.

Their relationship continued for another three months and included many more shared weekends at their respective residences. Though they did everything high school couples would do in the back seat of a car, the one thing they did not do was "it." Finally, Sheila, who was more than ready, asked Mark if there was a problem. He confessed that he had been on several blood pressure medications which made it difficult if not impossible to achieve an erection. He was embarrassed by his condition and said he tried Viagra and other pills but nothing worked. He professed his love for her and proposed marriage. She said yes and they were married for two years before she filed for divorce. Though there were times that they were able to have sex, she was not fulfilled and his problem in the bedroom had become one of those subjects that you never talk about but is always there. As a result, they found other issues to fight about which led to the breakdown of their marriage.

LEGALLY SPEAKING! When a client contacts our office for an annulment, we politely explain that you must have specific grounds for an annulment. One of those reasons is if the marriage was never consummated. In plain English that means the parties never had sex. In my thirty years of practicing law, I have never filed with the court a petition for annulment citing such a reason. That is not to say that I have not had numerous cases where things were not working out like they should have been in the bedroom and the failure to satisfy a marital partner has led to the demise of the marriage.

♛ IS HE A SWITCH HITTER?

In addition to making sure your partner's equipment works, you want to assure yourself that the person you are marrying is sexually oriented to be attracted to you. That's right. You are correct in understanding the last sentence. Even though our society has finally opened its minds to accepting that two people of the same sex should be allowed to enjoy the same benefits as a heterosexual couple, there are still people who will enter into a marriage knowing they are gay.

So how do you know if the person you are romantically involved with may really prefer someone of the same sex? This is especially confusing when she is great in bed or he gets aroused and you are both satisfied. The answer is never obvious and the truth most often surfaces after you have exchanged vows at the altar. But there are some clues to look for. Consider the following story:

ROSEANNE AND PETER'S STORY"
"THE FATHER OF MY TWO CHILDREN WAS GAY!"

Roseanne and Peter married when they were both in their late twenties after dating for two years. Both came from very religious backgrounds and had done little dating before they met each other. Almost immediately Roseanne became pregnant. Within three years they had two children. Roseanne said their sex life was okay though she usually initiated sex which she did not feel comfortable doing. Though Mike never turned down her advances, she said it always seemed mechanical.

When Roseanne looked back upon the time before they were married, she remembered that her husband had a few male friends but they never had girlfriends. When Roseanne and Peter announced to their family and friends that they were getting married, she thought it was kind of strange that Peter's friends suddenly disappeared and none of them came to the wedding. She was also angry at some of her girlfriends who kidded her about whether Peter was straight. She discounted all such talk as garbage and jealousy as she was the first of her friends to get married.

But soon after the second child was born, Peter seemed more distant. He worked later hours or would have a "drink with the guys after work." Finally, suspecting that he was having an affair, she confronted him. He was having an affair but not with another woman. Peter admitted he was gay but that he was shamed into getting married by his domineering parents.

The previous story is surely not to be used as a scientific measure of testing one's sexuality. It does give some insight into subtle clues that may raise enough doubt as to whether the person you are marrying is the person he or she really is.

LEGALLY SPEAKING! When one of the parties to a marriage makes a material misrepresentation to the other as to his sexual preference, such misrepresentation would be sufficient grounds for an annulment.

⚜ DON'T BE FOOLED BY THE OUTSIDE WRAPPING

From very early on in life, boys are dressed in blue and girls in pink. Boys play with trucks while girls are given dolls. But just because the wrapping on the outside blinks male or female, that does not guarantee what is inside the package. Therefore, when considering a second trip down the aisle, don't' be fooled by the wrapping and inspect the contents carefully.

STEVEN'S STORY
"HIS WIFE LOVED ANOTHER WOMAN!"

My client Steven wished that he had followed this advice but was too madly in love to do so. He was forty and never married before. Connie was in her late thirties when they met. She had a brief marriage right out of college. Unfortunately, Steven's blindness for love prevented him from seeing there was another person in Connie's life; her best friend Amy. From the time Steven and Connie met, Amy was always there. She and Connie were best friends. When Connie and Steve announced they were getting married, Connie joked to him that, "Wouldn't it be funny if Amy came along on their honeymoon."

Before marriage, Steven accepted the closeness of Connie and Amy's relationship. He grew up with sisters and knew how tight they were with their best friends. But after marriage, he became jealous. It seemed that any plans he made, Connie wanted to include Amy. Frequently, Amy would come by uninvited. When Connie became pregnant, she seemed more involved with the baby's arrival than her friendship with Amy which made Steven happier. Unfortunately, once the baby was born all that changed. It was as if there were two mothers and no room for Dad. Steven finally confronted his wife who admitted she had feelings for Amy that went beyond friendship.

CHAPTER NINETEEN

In my thirty years of practice, I can count on one hand the number of times that men cried in my office. Steven was one of them. He was so upset and confused. He continuously asked me, "How could I be so stupid? How could I have not known?"

PRACTICAL POINT: A man can compete with another guy for the love of a woman. But he will always lose out to another woman. Before you become blinded by love, you must especially listen to persons around you who may be more objective while you are acting on emotion. In Steven's case, his friends told him something was up. Amy had never married or even dated. But Steven ignored his friends'(friend's) questions which ultimately became his biggest mistake. For a further discussion, see Chapter Twelve, Listening to the *Voices of Public Opinion.*

Ch 20

Risky Business

Okay, so his health is good and he checks out in the bedroom. However, before you say I do, again, does he bring a financial risk to your future stability?

♛ GREAT SEX ALONE DOESN'T PAY THE BILLS

Money is the one thing couples say they argue about the most. Bill problems are often ranked at the top as the number one reason why people divorce. Regardless of this alarming statistic, it is so easy to be blinded by love and not see or sometimes not want to see the important issues. No matter how great the relationship might be, it doesn't pay the bills once you are married. That is why it is essential that you evaluate the financial stability of your partner before taking a second trip down the aisle.

Consider the following:

- Is he late in paying his bills?
- Is he drowning in debt?
- Is he being sued for a debt he owes?
- Does he owe federal and/or state income taxes?
- Has he asked you to borrow money?
- Does he mismanage money?
- Does he spend beyond his means?

Whether your future spouse is sexier than Brad Pitt or Angelina Jolie, a person's financial habits will not be different once you get married. No matter how nice your bank, landlord, or company that financed your car is, an IOU is not an acceptable form of payment.

Therefore, if you are frugal and good with money and he is not, then money is going to be a major source of conflict in your marriage. Unless you have won the lottery, after the excitement of the honeymoon has worn off, you will begin to resent the fact that you are always bailing out your spouse for his financial mistakes.

♛ DOING YOUR DUE DILIGENCE

If you are an heir to the Hilton or Walton fortune, then you do not have to work. Likewise, it is not important whether your partner has a job or not. Instead, you can both sail around the world on your one hundred foot yacht, sipping champagne and making love as you watch the sunset. STOP!!! It's time to get back to the real world.

Very, very few of us live in that world. For the rest, we have to work and often work extremely hard to meet our obligations. When bills start to pile up, it creates financial stress on a marriage. Entering into a marriage without fully knowing the financial health of your partner often leads to divorce.

As marriage is a partnership, before deciding if you want this person to be your partner, you need to conduct an investigation. In legal terms, conducting an investigation before you decide whether to move forwar,d is known as doing your due diligence. If you were buying a car, you want to know if it has been in an accident and whether the engine has been maintained. If you were hiring a person for employment, you would want references. Contemplating marriage should be no different. If you con-clude that it is not a good deal, you should walk away and look for a better opportunity.

PRACTICAL POINT: So you think you've met the person of your dreams. She is kind and sweet. He loves your kids. But will this union lead to financial harmony or result in financial discord? In beginning your investigation, it is best to be honest and explain to your intended why you want this information and that you want this to be mutual so that both sides can evaluate each other's financial condition. This way it will not appear as if you are prejudging his or her financial responsibility.

ROBIN'S STORY

Robin had been married only six months to Dave. She had sold her home from her first marriage and put her share of the profits into a joint account with Dave as they were planning to buy a condo. One day, when opening the mail, she received a letter from their bank. Their checking account had been attached and any remaining funds were frozen.

When she called the bank, she was told that the action was a result of one of Dave's creditors who had obtained a judgment and was now attempting to enforce it. Robin was aware that Dave had some old bills but he had assured her he was working on paying them off. Even after she confronted him that night, he was not completely honest failing to tell her about other accounts that had already sued him.

After consulting a bankruptcy attorney, they learned they did not qualify to file. As a result, they ended up paying the almost $50,000 debt which wiped out almost all of Robin's savings. Robin felt betrayed by her husband's deceit and depressed that she would be living in an apartment for the foreseeable future. Dave's financial issues overshadowed any attempt to get their marriage back on track. Robin eventually filed for divorce.

Robin's biggest mistake was putting her money into a joint account with her husband. Had she checked out Dave's credit before marriage by doing her due diligence, she may have reconsidered her pending marriage. Sure, doing an investigation does sound cold and selfish, and definitely not romantic. But getting stuck paying bills is not sexy either.

When considering marriage for a second time you should know as much as you can about your partner before going into business. If the person is saddled with debt with no reasonable way out for the foreseeable future, he or she is not a good investment of your time and probably your money! Instead, walk away.

SALLY'S STORY

Sally and Frank had a lot in common when they met at a school function for their children; they each had been married before, worked in related fields, and enjoyed the same types of food.

After only nine months of dating, Frank popped the question to which Sally immediately said yes. Two months into their marriage she had wished she said, "I need to ask some questions." In turns out that Frank was involved in a lawsuit that resulted from a business he had with a friend. The case was soon going to court and his attorney was asking for a substantial retainer fee. Even worse, if Frank lost, he would have to sell his home in order to satisfy the judgment.

If your fiancé reveals he is being sued, or has other financial problems, you should consult with an attorney to learn how any debts may affect you in the event your spouse later passes away, becomes disabled, or if the two of you divorce. You should also seek the advice of an attorney who does not represent your fiancé as he may be biased in his opinion of the case.

♛ ROMANCE AND THE GOOD, THE BAD, AND THE UGLY

You have met the man of your dreams and he is perfect in every way. He is someone who shares your same values and goals, and you want to spend the rest of your life with. Even better, he is nothing like your Ex.

Before you start working on the invitation list, this is the time to invite him to your own financial examination. Though it's not fun taking the romance out of a second marriage, especially if you're fortunate to find true love the second time around, remarriage doesn't get any easier. Whether you're divorced or widowed, you will still be dealing with many of the same issues. So be smart when it comes to love, and you'll enjoy your second chance at it that much more.

PRACTICAL POINT: Such conversations should occur when the relationship has reached the point where marriage is being discussed. Obviously, if you are simply having fun and you know it is not going anywhere, no sense getting off the ride before it's over. But if the relationship has passed the "newness" stage, before you hire the wedding planner and make a guest list, you want to make sure your intended is the one.

♛ A LOOK INSIDE A CREDIT REPORT

Credit reports include information about consumers that is obtained from creditors, collection agencies, and governmental agencies. The information contained will date back as much as ten years and will include the following:
- All first and last names used by the consumer as well as the names of persons he may be or was associated with as in the case of a present or former marriage

- All information of public record including judgments and tax liens
- Monies owed to governmental agencies for child support and alimony
- Bankruptcy filings
- A listing of all creditors both paid in full and outstanding

Note, along with the name of the creditor, the report will also provide any amount owed as well as whether the account has been paid on time or is late and if the account has been assigned to collection.

The report will also verify current employment and list reportable employment for the last ten years. Finally, it will also provide residential addresses of the person whose information is reported for.

LEGALLY SPEAKING! To obtain a credit report, you must provide the social security number of the person you are seeking information about. Furthermore, you cannot obtain a report about another without that person's written consent.

♛ FICO SCORES AND REMARRIAGE

Though your left brain is out shopping for dresses, your right brain needs to sit down with Mr. Wonderful and talk FICO scores. That's right. You need to know what his credit history is so that you are fully informed as to what you may be inheriting. Remember, the vows you take are for richer or poorer, not for poorer than before!

FICO is the acronym for the Fair Isaac Corporation, the company that generates credit scores. It is an individual's score that is used to determine how credit worthy that person is. The score is based on past credit history including whether you pay your bills on time or if you have been late. Having a low score is a red flag for lenders and should as well send up a warning flag to you.

Note, searching online is a great place to start. There are many web sites that will provide a credit report that pulls information from Experian, Trans Unio,n and Equifax which are the three leading credit reporting agencies. Chances are that, if there has been anything negative reported against a person's credit, it will show up on this report.

PRACTICAL POINT: Though some web sites charge a fee, look for a site that offers a free report.

♛ WHY IS IT IMPORTANT TO KNOW THE SCORE?

It has been proven that people who manage their finances in a responsible manner tend to also conduct other important aspects of their lives wisely. Arguably, the Chairman of the Board of General Electric has not had recent personal credit problems. Likewise, would you want to trust your brother with managing your money if he has bill problems? Of course not. Therefore, you should know how financially responsible the person who may become the manager of your money is before you invest in your future.

FICO scores don't lie and are a transparent look at:

- how we conduct our money life
- how much credit we use
- how much we owe
- how promptly we repay our loans
- how much we repay at a time
- how many late charges we incur
- what is our interest rate and
- how many credit cards do we owe on

PRACTICAL POINT: Consider this. If his FICO score is low, banks may not give him a loan to buy a car, let alone a loaf of bread. Therefore, before you say I do again, consider Mr. FICO as being another voice of public opinion!

SPECIAL SITUATION—HE HAS BEEN MARRIED BEFORE

If your fiancé has been married before, he may have unresolved financial issues concerning his prior marriage. These may include:

- Unpaid child and/or spousal support (alimony)
- Unpaid child and/or spousal support where his wages are not being garnished
- Seizure of assets to enforce unpaid child and/or spousal support
- Unresolved division of property issues
- A lowered credit score due to joint obligations still owed by him and his Ex

As a future partner to your fiancé, you have an absolute right to know everything about his financial past. After you have had an opportunity to evaluate the information provided, you will be able to make an informed decision as to whether you wish to say I do, again.

> **PRACTICAL POINT:** Newer marriages that carry financial and legal baggage from a previous relationship will quickly overshadow the romance that you are trying to build and perpetuate. Having an honest and open discussion about financial issues long before you exchange your vows will help assure a successful remarriage.

> **LEGALLY SPEAKING!** When a court dissolves the marriage but maintains jurisdiction over unresolved issues, it is said to "bifurcate" the marriage." By doing so, the parties are free to marry again. To illustrate, perhaps all of the property has not been divided or the court has not ruled on custody, or the amount of support. In these cases, the court can dissolve the marriage known as "bifurcation" but maintain jurisdiction over the case to resolve the remaining issues at a later time. Accordingly, before you say I do again, make sure that all your fiancé's issues have been resolved as you want your new marriage to begin with no baggage.

♕ SPECIAL PROBLEM—DEALING WITH YOUR FIANCE'S EX

It is only natural to dislike the person who may have treated your fiancé so terribly. But unless the Ex has passed away, he or she will almost always have some effect on your remarriage.

However, in dealing with the Ex, the best advice is to let your fiancé resolve any issues without your direct assistance. Though you may feel tempted to jump in and rescue your fiancé if you see him/her being upset by this person from their past, it's not your place.

Of course it is human nature to want to protect someone we love. If you hear screaming coming from the other end of the phone or watch your fiancé break down after a conversation with his Ex, it's going to upset you. Even though you do not want to see this person hurt, you may be doing more damage if you try to interfere into a situation that would be best you stay out of. This is especially true when it is about money. The best advice is to support him by offering advice but do not offer to doing the fighting for him.

PRACTICAL POINT: Dealing with the Ex-spouse is something your fiancé needs to sort out on his own in order to leave that chapter of his life behind and be able to start a new life with you. This is part of the healing your fiancé needs to do in order to be fully ready to marry you. Remember that the opposite of love is NOT hate! Both of those are very strong emotions. The opposite of love is apathy. It's when your partner reaches the point where they just don't get bothered by the things their ex does any more.

During those difficult times, there is a lot you can do which includes:
- Supporting your partner by offering advice but do not take an active role
- Bring to the attention of your fiancé the things the Ex is doing that he or she may not see
- Suggest a different approach to handling the situation
- Be a good listener

WARNING SIGNS!!!

The following are red flag financial warning signs about your fiancé that are telling you to proceed with caution:

Does your intended spouse:

- Have a credit score that is less than what you scored on the SAT Exam?
- Receive mail and phone calls from collection agencies?
- Not open his mail?
- Owe back child support?
- Overspend and shop all the time without giving any thought whatso-ever if he/she can afford it?
- Owe money to parents, siblings, or friends that are long over due?
- Not have a checking account?
- Cash his paycheck instead of depositing it in a bank?
- Survive on short-term "payday" loans?

JESSE'S STORY

Jesse thought she had met the perfect man. He was kind, good looking, romantic, and showered her with lavish gifts. From designer handbags to sunglasses, her husband loved buying her presents. He was equally kind to himself often walking into their home with shopping bags filled with new clothes. His free spending was nothing new as from the time of their second date, he was extremely generous.

Unfortunately Jesse was too caught up in the lifestyle to have questioned Rob before they got married as to how he paid his bills. He was salaried, made a decent living, but did not appear to be on the fasttrack to becoming a rising star in his company. Her first tip off of financial irresponsibility was when he would visit the ATM on almost every date. Too caught up in love, she ignored this warning sign. Within a year of the marriage, with mounting credit card debts and no money left to borrow on his cards, Rob announced that they had to file bankruptcy. Now, after all the years of her building her good credit, it was ruined. They subsequently filed for divorce.

LEGALLY SPEAKING: Money issues are the root of many marital problems and that goes double in second marriages. Therefore, you must approach a second marriage like any financial agreement you enter into so that you protect your money.

♛ A BRIDE'S WORST SCENARIO

If the above warnings haven't scared you away from the altar, consider what happened to one of my clients who failed to do her due diligence.

KIM'S STORY

Kim met Gary at a bar. They were both divorced and quickly realized they had a lot in common. They began dating which included many weekend trips to Las Vegas. Kim admitted she was impressed with Gary's high roller lifestyle as the hotels often awarded him many perks, including free hotel rooms and complimentary dinners. Kim never questioned his finances as he always seemed to have money. Though he lost at the table more often than he won, the hotels were eager to invite him back.

After a year, she moved into Gary's apartment. She did wonder why Gary had a post office box for his mail but accepted his answer that because he lived in a large apartment complex, his mail was often delivered to the wrong address. He also told her that bill collectors were always looking for his Ex wife and that if anyone ever came to the apartment looking for him, she should deny knowing where he was.

Kim however got the shock of her life when, at their wedding reception, a man dressed as a guest walked up to Gary, and handed him a stack of papers. In front of her friends, he said that Gary was being served for a debt he owed to a casino. In fact, Gary had owed many Vegas casinos thousands of dollars. Though, the couple had their first dance, as it turned out, it ended up being their last as well. I can only imagine what their wedding night was like!

♛ FINANCIAL CHECKLIST BEFORE YOU SAY I DO, AGAIN

Sometime, before the big day, you and your fiancé need to sit down and do a "show and tell" of your financial state of being. This should include disclosure of all:

✓ Debts secured by real estate
✓ Debts secured by cars, boats, and other motor vehicles
✓ Installment debts for major purchases such as electronics, furniture, and jewelry
✓ Credit cards
✓ Student loans
✓ Obligations owing for taxes (state and federal, real property)
✓ Disclosure of any court ordered debts for child support and alimony
✓ Liens
✓ Stipulated agreements (judgments) to pay

Financial questions to ask your fiancé before you say I do, again:
• Would you best describe yourself as someone who saves or someone who spends?
• Do you live on a budget?
• Do you balance your checkbook?
• Do you pay your bills on time?
• Have you ever bounced a check?
• Do you consider having a vacation every year a necessity or a luxury?
• Have you ever filed for bankruptcy?
• Have you ever had a creditor turn you over to a collection agency?
• Have you ever been sued?
• Has your bank account ever been attached by a creditor who you owed money to?
• Have your wages ever been garnished for payment of a debt?
• Have you started a business that later failed?
• Do you have any outstanding court fines?
• (If previously married) Do you owe any back child support? Have your wages ever been garnished for back support?

THE SYMPTOMS OF DIVORCE—WHAT YOU MAY HAVE MISSED THE FIRST TIME AROUND

"You know the honeymoon is pretty much over when you start to go out with the boys on Wednesday nights, and so does she."

The following discussion would have been most beneficial for you to read while you were still married to your Ex. But a Monday morning quarterback does not score any points. Regardless, recognizing the symptoms of divorce may help avoid a full outbreak of the disease.

Once a year I see my doctor for an annual physical. Fortunately, the examination has always been routine because I have not had any medical problems. Regardless, my doctor always asks me a series of questions such as, do I have any chest discomfort or difficulty breathing, digestion problems, have I gained or lost any weight, or have any difficulty with urination. Since I turned fifty a few years ago, the number of questions has increased. But regardless, a doctor is a diagnostician and he is looking for any symptoms that might lead to a diagnosis of a medical condition.

Of course, your doctor is often dependent upon you to tell him of any concerns that you may have. Likewise, he may have a difficult time discovering it on his own without some clues from you.

In a marriage, it is often said, "No one knows you better than your spouse." Well, that makes sense because you spend the majority of your time together and, unless you are running a covert operation for the CIA, husbands and wives are living as one. Of course we each have our own individuality but a wife knows her husband's favorite sweatshirt that he won't throw out no matter what, just like a husband knows her favorite restaurant.

In the same way, when a spouse begins to act differently than his normal pattern of behavior, this may be the beginning of subtle symptoms of a problem. Like the common cold, the sneezing and runny nose goes away after a few days. However, a symptom that persists and is left untreated rarely corrects itself. To illustrate, a spouse who was always there to pick the kids up after soccer practice on his way home, but is now working late every evening is raising a red flag warning there is an underlying problem. This symptom, if left untreated, could spell problems for the marriage.

In conducting interviews with clients, I have listened to the "symptoms" often given for why one spouse wanted to leave the marriage. The following were the most common:

- "We were spending less and less time together."
- "My life felt unfulfilled, there was so much more I wanted to do."
- "I was feeling depressed or uptight when going home, or not looking forward to going home."
- "We were having less fun when we were together, and time together has become more serious."
- "He was very bossy and always had to be right."
- "My opinion meant nothing!"
- "He had a drinking problem before we married which only got worse."
- "He paid attention to everyone but me."
- "As the years passed, it was evident that we wanted different things and had different needs so we grew further apart."
- "She became emotionally and sexually involved with someone else."
- "She was spending more money on "frivolous" unnecessary things and not caring to save for the future."
- "His worked consumed him and there was no time left for me."
- "Our marriage was never the same after we had kids."
- "When we were arguing, we were verbally attacking each other rather than really listening to one another."
- "I felt put down or taken for granted, or I was doing that to my

spouse."
- "There were increased periods of silence between and my spouse and I."
- "I had less and less sexual desire."
- "We never seemed to have the money to do things we needed to do."
- "I was making judgments alone or misreading what my spouse wanted to do."
- "I was losing my own identity as an individual."
- "I became confused about where we were going and often talked about "I" not "We.""

When questioned further, many clients were able to offer more specific signs or symptoms that something was different or changing in their relationship. Too often, when these symptoms are not addressed or left untreated, they result in irreparable harm to the marriage. As a result, divorce often becomes the only solution. But had these symptoms been recognized earlier, and treated, a marriage may have been saved.

If you or your fiancé have any of the above symptoms, it is wise to seek treatment now and before you say I do, again.

RISK FACTORS AND REMARRIAGE

In medicine, we know that certain disease carrying genes, and if inherited, can be passed on to children. To illustrate, if your parents and grandparents developed diabetes later in life, there is a good likelihood that you too will develop this disease and therefore at a higher risk than someone else. Likewise, psychologists have discussed how certain characteristics are a product of learned behavior when we are children and this behavior may follow us into adulthood.

The American Academy of Matrimonial Lawyers (AAML) released a study in 2004 identifying the top five reasons people get divorced: financial difficulties, poor communication, lack of commitment, mid-life crisis or major change in priorities, and marital infidelity. They have also identified several other important reasons for marriage failure, such as physical abuse, substance abuse, or gambling. The study explained these last three reasons as learned behavior when we were children and this behavior may follow us into adulthood.

The same study included factors shown to be associated with increased risk of divorce:

- If one or more of your or his parents were abusive to their spouse
- If one or more of your or his parents had an addiction problem
- Neuroticism
- Having children from a previous relationship
- If you and your fiancé are living together
- If your or his parents were divorced
- If he had a prior marriage
- If you and your fiancé have known each other for less than two years before remarriage
- If you and him have religious differences

Risk factors increase the likelihood of a failed marriage and have been proven to be an even greater risk to remarriage. Accordingly, review the above list of risk factors to determine if you or your fiancé carry the gene. This may help in your decision of whether to say I do, again.

Allison's Story

James' parents were Lutheran though he had not seen the inside of a church since he was a young boy. Allison's parents observed the Jewish holidays. The two never talked about religion before marriage. During the early years of their marriage, Allison would go alone to temple and to her parents for the Jewish holidays. Though she always resented that James would not support her, she never conveyed her feelings to him. She also never saw her choice for practicing her faith as religious but one of tradition.

They had two children. When their son was about to turn thirteen, Allison expressed her wishes that she wanted him to have a Bar Mitzvah. To Allison's surprise, James was adamantly opposed. He said that he did not want that for his son and "there would be no more discussion." A few days later, he came home and presented his son with a crucifix to wear around his neck.

James and Allison continued to argue and eventually sought counseling which did not help. Their disagreement over how their children should be raised religiously overshadowed their entire marriage and eventually the parties separated.

❦ MULTIPLE MARRIAGES IN HIS PAST

A guy slices his ball in the woods and goes to look for it. He meets a girl from the next fairway who is looking for her ball. They start to chat and have a wonderful conversation. She suddenly says to him, "You know...you look like my third husband." He says, "Oh yeah," and then asks her how many times she has been married?" "Twice," she replies.

What is it about marriage that people don't want to give up trying to make it work? Instead some keep remarrying and remarrying. Remember the expression,

"If you throw something up in the air enough times, eventually it is going to stick."

Well this is not always the case with marriage. If your fiancé has had several past marriages, this may be a warning sign that he is not marriage material.

BILL'S STORY

Bill was a national sales training manager. He met Pam on a business trip and they began a long distance relationship. Because of Bill's work, he was able to see Pam at least once a month. After a few months, he also arranged for her to fly out to visit him.

Bill was never married before and Pam acknowledged having three prior marriages. Bill, blinded by love and great sex, failed to ask Pam why the previous nuptials failed and within a year they were married.

Soon thereafter he realized what he had in common with the Ex husbands. Pam was, in his words, "a bitch." She was self-absorbed only caring for herself except that she did have a keen interest in his checkbook. Bill also used adjectives such as moody, detached, and mean to describe Pam. Ironically, once the ring was on her finger, the great sex that he enjoyed came to a sudden stop.

Had Bill heeded the warning signs before he said I do, this marriage could have been prevented. For a man and woman to stay together as husband and wife, they have to at least like each other. The fact that Pam had multiple marriages should send a clear signal that perhaps it was not always the Ex spouse's fault. It is most important to find out as much information about past marriages and engagements to see if there is a pattern.

FACTOID: Studies have shown that persons who have had multiple marriages or engagements are also more likely to have problems with substance abuse, mental health problems, poverty or family violence that predispose them to more unstable lives, no matter which marriage they were in. Additionally, the National Council of Family Relations reports that men who remarry for a third time have a subsequent divorce rate of more than 80 percent. For women who have had more than two marriages, the divorce rate is over 70 percent.

♛ A FREQUENT MARRIAGE CHECKUP

Has your fiancé had several prior marriages or engagements? His answers to the following questions may give you further insight into the person you are about to marry:

- ✓ For each marriage, how long were you married?
- ✓ What was the reason each marriage ended in divorce?
- ✓ Who initiated each divorce proceeding?
- ✓ Were you ever engaged to anyone who you did not eventually marry?
- ✓ (If so) Why did you not get married?
- ✓ Are your parents divorced?
- ✓ Were they married before?
- ✓ Have any of your siblings been married, divorced, and remarried?

REBECCA'S STORY

Rebecca's first marriage was shortly after high school and she said it, "didn't really count." Her second marriage followed a few years later and lasted even less. With her third marriage came her two children. Now divorced three times, and with two kids with needs that were not being fulfilled by the small and infrequent amount of child support she was receiving from husband number three, she decided to market herself and go for number four.

Burt was a traveling salesperson who met Rebecca at a conference they were both attending. Drinks that night led to dinner the next, followed by an all expense vacation that Burt paid for to fly Rebecca out to California. Within six months, Rebecca had entered "Multiple Remarry Land" which involved moving herself and two children across the country and settling into southern California.

With her bills being paid, groceries in the refrigerator, and new clothes for the kids, all seemed to be going fine until one day when Rebecca took off her rose colored glasses and realized that Burt and her Ex spouses all shared the same problem that led her into Divorce Land; he like the others was addicted to gambling. His gambling was not confined to a friendly poker game either. No. Instead, Burt was playing the horses, running up big tabs at the crap tables in Vegas, and betting the farm (in this case the house) on Sunday afternoon football.

Finally, after months of begging him to seek help, and with the roof over their heads literally about to be lifted, she filed divorce number four. In consultation, Rebecca admitted that her problem was that she married instead of dating never getting to know the person before saying I do!

GETTING TO KNOW YOU

How well do you and your fiancé know each other? Are you completely at ease being around him or walk as though you are stepping on egg shells? Is he relaxed around you? Before you answer too quickly, consider whether the two of you are in the "comfort zone."

The comfort zone is that stage of a relationship when both spouses no longer have to work hard to impress each other. He already knows your little quirks and you have discovered his pet peeves. He may be leaving his dirty socks on the floor or not putting up the toilet seat. He may even feel comfortable farting in front of you. (I could have said passing wind but I am in my comfort zone).

Regardless, there comes a time in a relationship where both of you agree that you have dated each other long enough and want to take it to the next level. But before you push the button on the Wedding Express elevator, consider the following questions. Keep in mind each question ends with the phrase:

"without fearing he will storm out of the room and call off the relationship."

1. Can you offer objective criticism without fearing he will storm out of the room and call the relationship off?
2. Can you say No to him . . . . . .?
3. Can you tell him he's wrong . . . . . . ?
4. Can you hurt his feelings . . . . . . ?
5. Can you kidd(joke with) him about his parents, siblings . . . . . . ?
6. Can you discuss your political or religious views . . . . . . ?

PRACTICAL POINT: Marriage is all about open communication. Likewise, when one or both spouses fear how what they say or do may be perceived by the other, will spend their marriage defending their actions. In contemplating remarriage, take a personal inventory of whether you were open with your Ex. Note, statistics show that couples who are open in their communication and expression stand a much better chance of seeing their second marriage succeed.

♕ DON'T BE FOOLED BY THE PERSON STANDING AT THE ALTAR

Certain patterns of behavior may be subtle signs of a problem that may only get worse once that ring is on your finger.

LAURIE'S STORY

Laurie and Dan dated for only nine months before they got married. Dan was never married before, though Laurie had a brief marriage that lasted only six months.

During the months leading up to the wedding day, Laurie was often teased by Dan's friends who asked her if "she had ever seen Dan's dark side" referring to his temper. Laurie would always laugh off the questions.

However, while attending an Angel baseball game with another couple, Dan became irate when leaving the parking lot. Apparently, a car pulled out in front of him. The other driver then glared at Dan. Dan immediately bolted out of his car blocking the other driver who had moved only a few feet. He then went to the driver's door shouting obscenities while he tugged on the door handle to open the door. Though Dan's friend tried to pry him away, it was to no avail. A security guard saw what was happening and finally brought the incident to a halt.

Though Laurie was frightened and remembered his friend's warnings, she still kept her appointment to walk down the aisle. Within one year of marriage, she was in our office crying. She was a victim of constant verbal abuse and felt foolish that she ignored the warning signs.

What at first may seem illogical about divorce is the fact that at one time there was an extremely happy couple walking down the aisle in marital bliss. How is it then that over time one's personality could have been so altered so much that he is now this ugly monster or she is a cold, selfish bitch. We have all heard that she got divorced because "he was not the same man she married," or that "she was great when we dated, but she changed."

The truth is that marriage doesn't change people. What you see standing at the altar is not going to be any different five or ten years later. The question you must ask is whether you want to enter into a partnership with this person? To help answer your question, you will need to look into his/her past to find the answer for the future. Consider the following:

♛ BORN OF A FAMILY OF CHEATERS

It has often been said that we learn from our parents. They are our role models and our behavioral patterns as adults are shaped from what we observe as children. In a harmonious home, where parents show love and affection toward each other, this conduct would be viewed by a child as acceptable behavior. Likewise, a child who grows up in a home where his parents are unfaithful to each other, this may also be perceived as acceptable behavior when he becomes an adult.

FACTOID: Spouses who have extra-marital affairs are often products of parents who committed adultery in their marriages. Research has shown that where one or both parents have had extra-marital affairs, children of the marriage often acquire the same trait, and continue this behavior in their marriage.

ELLEN'S STORY

Ellen retained our services for a premarital agreement. It would be her second marriage. Her fiancé confided that his first marriage ended because he was guilty of having multiple affairs. But that was now "out of his system" and he was committed to his upcoming marriage. When Ellen questioned her fiancé about his childhood, she learned that his parents divorced when he was nine. Furthermore, his father abused alcohol, had affairs during the marriage, and had a subsequent failed remarriage.

PRACTICAL POINT: If the person you marry has been unfaithful in his first marriage, you will always doubt in your mind whether he is being faithful to you.

❦ WHEN A PAST RELATIONSHIP IS NOT OVER

Just because the divorce papers are signed does not always signal that the relationship is over. Especially when there are children involved, there will be continuous interaction with an Ex spouse. In most cases, this causes irritation for the new spouse. However, when contemplating marriage, you must make sure that the members from his or her previous relationship (relationships) are not still smoldering. Because if they are, any chance that the fire may be rekindled will almost always prove disastrous for you.

TERESA'S STORY

Teresa was ten years younger than her husband Jeff who was divorced with two children. The divorce was amicable and Jeff saw his boys every other weekend. His wife was also okay with Jeff coming over during the week to help them with their homework.

On those nights, Teresa would have dinner with a friend. However, after a year of marriage, the once a week homework tutoring session became two nights a week and Jeff was now sitting down for dinner with the family. Teresa became suspicious that maybe there was something more going on than just Math and Science homework but accepted Jeff's answer that he wanted to be a great father who spent quality time with his kids.

After another year of marriage, her suspicions were confirmed when Jeff announced that he wanted to separate without giving her any reason other than, "he needed his space to think." Not surprisingly, Jeff moved back into his Ex-wife's home.

❦ ALWAYS SECOND BEST

Do you know where you rank? That is, are you the number one most important person in your future spouse's eyes or will you be sharing that position with someone else? Even if you are not in the top spot, are you okay with it? Before you say I do, again, the two of you should feel secure in the relationship. Likewise, you deserve some assurance that your ranking may not continue to fall later on.

RONNIE'S STORY

Ronnie had grown children and had been divorced for several years when she met Rich. Rich too had been previously married with adult children.

When the two started dating, Ronnie thought it was awfully sweet that Rich was always checking in with his daughter to see how she was. However, as their relationship grew, Ronnie did think that the frequency of contact was a little odd as Rich would call his daughter at almost every opportunity which included times that were not opportune for Ronnie. However, she dismissed the relationship as a very concerned father for his adult unmarried daughter.

Wedding bells soon chimed for Ronnie and Rich. But so did the doorbell on their condo as the step-daughter became a frequent and often uninvited guest, at least she was not invited by Ronnie, to their home.

Finally, when Rich suggested that his daughter accompany them on a cruise, Ronnie questioned her husband's relationship with his daughter which infuriated him. After two years of marriage, Ronnie was definitely feeling second best and asked Rich to choose whether he wanted to be married to her or spend time with his daughter. She also stressed to him the relationship was no longer working. Rich was incensed by the suggestion that he instead chose to dissolve the marriage.

When considering remarriage, if you have any doubt as to where you stand now or where you may stand, it is time to hit the brakes on the remarriage until this issue is resolved. Ponder the following:

Is your spouse married to:
- his kids?
- his job?
- his friends?
- his parents?
- himself?

⚜ IN-LAWS MAKE STRANGE BED FELLOWS!

What if your spouse-to-be ranks you as number one, but your future in-laws are still rooting for his Ex? Though the vows that are exchanged are between a husband and wife, the influence exerted by an in-law can have an impact on the success of a remarriage. Consider the following:

ANNE'S STORY

Ann met Stuart before her divorce from her Ex was finalized though she had been separated for more than a year. After only a few dates, Stuart was anxious for her to meet his parents. Upon that first encounter, Stuart's mother was pleasant but made a point of telling Ann how wonderful Stuart's wife was and how she is still "very good friends" With her. As Stuart had children with his Ex, Ann rationalized that his Mom needed to keep a friendly relationship so that it would not hinder her ability to see her grandchildren on a regular basis.

However, throughout the courtship, his Mom continued to compare Ann with Stuart's Ex and the comparisons were not always complimentary to Ann. Nevertheless, Ann and Stuart proceeded with wedding plans as she believed that once married, Stuart's Mom would come around and embrace their relationship. Unfortunately, that did not happen. Finally, over a holiday dinner wherein the Mom went on and on about the wonderful lunch she had with the Ex, Ann stormed out of the room in tears. Stuart ran after his wife and then lectured his mother about how rude she had been. Following that evening, Stuart did not speak to his mother for the next year. However, the stress that was created put a strain on the marriage as Stuart felt he was choosing between his mother and wife. Before the next Christmas, the peace pipe was waved and the parties reconciled. However, Ann never felt that she was welcomed into the family.

♛ ARE YOU MARRYING A MOMMY'S BOY
   OR A DADDY'S LITTLE GIRL?

You're standing at the altar. As you are about to hear the words:

"I now pronounce you husband and wife," you sense that something is terribly wrong. But, instead of shouting STOP, you stare adoringly into the eyes of your fiancé who will become your husband in another nanosecond. As you do, you notice that his eyes are fixed on his mother. You feel flushed and want to scream but your voice box is paralyzed. The nanosecond then passes and as you and your husband face your family and friends and take those first steps into married life you are wondering what was that all about.

Sounds crazy? Well, as hard as it is to imagine, I personally witnessed this at a wedding several years ago. While the marriage has survived, the bride continues to compete with her mother-in- law for her husband's affection. Accordingly, before you say I do, again, paying close attention to his family relationships may provide you insight into your future with your partner.

♛ THE UMBILICAL CHORD HAS NEVER BEEN CUT!

Mothers and Dads share a special bonding with their sons and daughters. As young children some of us might remember when Dad was upset with Jack only to hear Mom come to his defense. Or perhaps Mom and Jill were fighting over something obscure and Dad always sided with his daughter. Such relationships are special and for those of us who have lost a parent, I am sure you would like to have one more minute with your parents.

As we grow into adulthood, it is the normal maturation process for parents to let their children spread their wings and develop their own identity. Of course it is okay to call Mom and Dad when a problem arises or just to get advice. Likewise, they should always be there for you. But when you walk down the aisle, the person you have chosen to marry you should be the one you first turn to for support.

JANET'S STORY

Janet was married only one year to Jim when he died of inoperable stomach cancer. They were high school sweethearts and Jim was the only man she ever dated. The last thing she wanted to do was start dating again. However, at the begging of a male co-worker, she agreed to a blind date with Alan. Alan was never married and was six years older than her.

She said her first date was a lot of fun and the two agreed to see each other again. After two months, she met Alan's parents and immediately thought it was a little odd how involved his mother was in his life. She would bring his car in for repairs, buy his clothes, and called the dentist when he needed his teeth cleaned. She even made all the arrangements when Alan took her away to Las Vegas for the weekend.

But Janet was convinced that once they were married, Alan would become more independent. Unfortunately, just the opposite took place. Alan wanted Mom to come with them to look for furniture, to purchase a new car, and more. When the talk came about starting a family, Janet had fears that her mother-in-law would be parked in her house everyday with Mom and her new baby.

The previous example is not intended to send the message that part of marriage includes divorcing yourself from your parents. Absolutely not as your parents should always be part of your life. Needless to say, the person you marry should be able to balance his or her relationship with you and his parents. It is not a matter of taking sides as there are no sides here.

♛ WARNINGS SIGNS OF A MOMMY'BOY OR DADDY'S LITTLE GIRL

- Is his/her parent's involved in making every important decision?
- Do you have concerns that you will never be a part of the decision making process?
- Do you have concerns that your future spouse will not respect your opinion and will seek a second opinion from his parents?

HE WAS NEVER MARRIED BEFORE

Despite the saying that goes, "There is someone out there for everyone," not everyone finds that person by a certain age. Though statistically the median age for a first marriage is twenty-seven, some of us do not find that special person until later in life. Look at Jerry Seinfeld. He was forty-three when he married.

Marrying a person who has lived almost half his life single comes with challenges that are not seen in someone who has already been married before.

LUCIE'S STORY

Lucie met Luke in their third year of college and they were married shortly after graduating. The marriage lasted only two years as they both admitted they were too young. In contrast, she continued to excel at work and in only five years had been promoted to vice president of an employment staffing company.

With little time for serious dating, she was content with having fun with her friends and family. However, as she approached her thirtieth birthday, Lucie realized that she would like to meet someone and hopefully start a family.

Her girlfriend's husband introduced her to Larry. He was ten years older than her and had never been married. Larry owned his own home which was beautifully furnished. Within a few weeks, Lucie was telling her friends that she thought Larry was the one. They were married six months later and never lived together before. But it was after she said "I do," that the problems began. Larry had his daily routine and he was content eating alone without Lucie. If Lucie did not want to see a certain movie, he would announce that he was fine seeing it alone. She soon felt although two people lived in the home they had two distinct lives.

A person who has never been married may become more selfish and self-centered as he has only needed to care for himself. After so many years of not having to discuss with someone which restaurant to go to or what movie to see ,whether to make the bed or not, it is sometimes a huge adjustment to now be with someone who has their own opinions, likes, and dislikes.

Remarrying because your biological timeclock is ticking is discussed in Chapter Seven.

⚜ THE HAPPINESS FACTOR

"If you love what you do and love who you are with, you will never work a day in your life."

When I give advice to my kids, (they are twenty-nine and twenty-six, but in my eyes are still my babies) I always tell them that I am a big proponent of the happiness factor. That is, I don't care how much money you make or have, if you are not happy, it doesn't really matter how fat your checkbook is.

In researching for this book, I came across a study about long life and happiness. It concluded that people, regardless of what type of work they did, lived longer if they were happy during their lives. Whether your teachings have educated young minds or your skills have aided people to get well, you have achieved inner happiness.

The study also contrasted happiness and lack of happiness and marriage. In contrast to job satisfaction, people who were unhappy in their marriage did not perform as well on the job. This would seem to make sense as for most, marriage is work. When the marriage was not working, you were not happy and therefore the marriage ended. Unfortunately, too many clients have also told me that they have stayed in a marriage where they were miserable for too long only to one day wake up and realize they needed to move on. For most, the moving van should have arrived much sooner than it did.

In questioning nondivorce clients who were in long-term marriages, I asked them,

What is it that first attracted you to your spouse enough that you wanted to see them again?

The number one response offered by women was, "He made me laugh." That would seem logical because even if he looked like George Clooney but could not put two words together, it is doubtful that a meaningful relationship would ever develop.

As a follow up question, I asked,

Why did you continue to see him?

The most offered response from women was

"When I was with him, I felt happy."

In your first marriage, was that person you adoringly said I do to not turn out to be that special person who made you love every day of your marriage? Perhaps he was verbally abusive or hated your parents, or was selfish and indifferent.. Regardless of the reasons, you now deserve to love what you do and to do it with someone you love. The key is to find that right person the second time around.

Accordingly, before you say I do, again, consider what is it about your fiancé that caused you to want to continue dating. Most importantly, is that candle still burning or has the flame turned to just a flicker?

♛ DOES HE HAVE AN ADDICTIVE BEHAVIOR?

Did your Ex have an addictive behavior? Were you successful in getting him to change? Probably not. Therefore, if the person you are about to say I do to has a trait that is offensive to you, do not think he will quit once you are married. Despite how much he professes his love for you, he has to want to quit and there is nothing you can do to make it happen. Consider whether the following are deal breakers.

- He smokes
- He drinks too much
- He gambles
- He smokes pot
- He won't lose weight
- He won't exercise
- He's selfish

- He's cheap
- He spends the whole weekend watching sports
- He won't stop watching porn
- He won't go to church/synagogue with you

DENNIS'S STORY
"ADDICTED TO SEX"

Dennis met Diane at a club on a Friday night. She was there with a few of her girlfriends from work. After buying her a drink, he quickly learned that she was a single Mom and her son was out of state visiting his Dad.

After a few more drinks, it was obvious to all that Dennis was going home with Diane that night and he stayed all weekend long. By Sunday night, he had engaged in more sex in a forty-eight hour period than he had all year long. Things were pretty good outside of the bedroom, kitchen, living room, and car as Diane and Dennis's relationship grew. Finally, after six months, Dennis popped the question to which Diane screamed, "Yes."

But Dennis quickly discovered being married to Diane meant having to be ready to perform any time and all the time as Diane never seemed satisfied. Finally, after a year of feeling like a horse sent to a stud farm, Dennis confronted Diane and asked if she thought she had a problem. His question was greeted by Diane tugging Dennis' pant legs and pulling him into the bedroom. Before she could get his pants off, he asked the question again but this time it changed the mood as Diane started to cry.

Despite a brief attempt to seek help for sexual addiction, Diane fell back into bed with a co-worker. Thereafter, Dennis filed for divorce.

SPECIAL SITUATION: ARE YOU LOOKING FOR SHARED ADDICTIVE BEHAVIORS?

Are you attracted to your own addictive behavior? Consider Cher's story:

CHER'S STORY

Cher had been married twice before when she married Derek. In conversation, she told me he abused wine to the point where it became a substitute for food as he would drink heavily every night. When he did, he would go into an alcoholic rage where he became verbally abusive of Cher.

When she compared her three husbands, all her Ex's shared the same addictive behavior. Unfortunately, that is what attracted her to them as she also enjoyed wine to the point where she could not hold her alcohol and would often pass out.

❧ HE PROMISES TO TELL THE TRUTH, THE WHOLE TRUTH, AND NOTHING BUT THE TRUTH

Is your prospective spouse an honest person? Is there anything about him that causes you to question his credibility? When I meet a client and decide to take his case, part of my evaluation process includes whether he has a viable argument. But, equally as important, is whether the person comes off as being believable. This is because in the world of law, the person can have the strongest case but if no one believes him, he may still lose.

> PRACTICAL POINT: A successful marriage is based on truth and honesty. In counseling persons who are going through a divorce, when one spouse has been dishonest to the other, it is rather difficult for him to rebuild trust. As a result, often this lack of trust becomes a major stumbling block that eventually leads to the breakdown of the marriage.

BEN'S STORY

During the initial consultation for Estate Planning, I routinely ask my clients if they have had any prior marriages. This information is necessary so that I can determine if there are children who may be heirs of the Estate that may not be from the present marriage.

A few years back, clients who had to be well into their seventies were sitting in my office. When I asked the question, the wife smile and said that she and her husband were soon to be celebrating their fifty-fifth wedding anniversary. As I was about to circle on my form that there were no other marriages, the husband in a whispery voice announced that he had a six month marriage when he was eighteen and there was a child he had never seen after the divorce.

At that moment, the wife turned redder than the ripest tomato, picked up her purse, glared at her husband with her nostrils about to explode with a plume of fire, and walked out. The husband tried to utter some form of an apology but he too then left. Both clients were never to be heard from again despite our attempt to call their home and write a letter. We later learned that the wife went to live with her daughter.

You may say what was the harm of the husband making his confession after so many years? But to the wife, it did matter as she no longer could trust her husband. Of course she probably would have still married him fifty-five years ago had he told her then what she later found out. No matter how long you may be married, hearing a lie destroys the trust you have in one another. In contemplating marriage, the person you are about to exchange vows must pass your test of credibility. Accordingly, before you say I do again, consider asking the following questions:

♛ CHECKLIST TO HONESTY
Have you ever:

✓ been married?
✓ (if so) been unfaithful?
✓ had your marriage annulled?
✓ been engaged?
✓ had children?
✓ been arrested?
✓ served time in jail?
✓ been sued?
✓ filed bankruptcy?
✓ had a business failure?

♛ IS HE MARRYING YOU FOR TODAY OR FOR TODAY AND TOMORROW?
Is your fiancé trading up? The fact that he may consider you prettier and more exciting than his Ex does not mean that you have an indefinite shelf life. In fact, if this is a pattern for him, you too may be on the trading block in a few years.

SYMPTOMS OF "TRADING UP"
The condition of wanting to trade up typically occurs when one spouse's income increases exponentially due to a change in employment, promotion, timing, or just plain good fortune. Often, the other spouse is a homemaker and has worked little or no time outside the home since they were married. At first, both spouses are enjoying their newfound wealth. Soon however, the spouse whose income has improved may announce that he has more value than his spouse and wants to move on. In other situations, the spouse may meet someone and has or want to have an affair. These symptoms may occur at any time during a marriage but more common in

longer-term marriages and mostly affects forty plus males but has been seen in younger people.

A popular radio talk show host in Los Angeles boasts the fact that he has had several marriages that all ended in divorce therefore making him an expert on relationships. One of reasons he cites for why marriages fail is when a spouse (typically the male) wants to "trade up." In other words, his economic situation in life has dramatically and rapidly improved from the time he was first married. Likewise, he can now, because of his newfound wealth, attract a higher class female than what he married and he therefore wants to trade in the old for a new and improved model. Not surprisingly, the newer edition is usually much younger than whom she is replacing.

Over the years, clients (mostly men)(,) have appeared in our office repeatedly with the same scenario. All that changes is the year and the names. Regardless that his wife of many years continues to maintain the home and the lifestyle they were always accustomed to and comfortable with, he is willing to trade it all in for something new. Though, she has raised the family, the kids are older and her contributions now appear to have little value.

How does this happen? Well, with more money there are more opportunities to spend it and more opportunities to meet people a spouse may normally not meet when he was home every night doing homework with the kids. Now, his new job responsibilities require entertaining clients, attending company retreats, and business travel all to the exclusion of his wife. His home, once the centerpiece of their relationship where they enjoyed entertaining family and friends, has little attachment. The home simply becomes shelter, which he can also find at any Hilton or Hyatt Hotel.

SUSAN'S STORY

Susan's husband, Frank, was a district sales manager for a shoe company. They were high school sweethearts and had three girls. Frank's company went public and he was offered a national sales position. His salary, with bonuses, tripled after the first year. With the additional income, the older Ford and Toyota Camry were traded in for a new Mercedes and Lexus SUV, they joined a tennis club and took a Mediterranean cruise. As his income continued to increase, his family interests began to wane. He seemed distant from his wife though he kept telling her that he was tired from work. He was also spending less and less time at home and traveling more frequently. Susan chose to avoid talking to him about his changed personality hoping things would get back to the way they use to be. But when he confronted her about decisions she made, he would put her down saying she doesn't understand business. The few times he would agree to socialize with their friends, he would embarrass her saying she was lucky enough to graduate high school. This went on for over a year. Finally, after enduring more humiliation than she could take, Susan decided to end her marriage of twenty-seven years.

LEGALLY SPEAKING! In states that require the proving of specific grounds for divorce, Frank's conduct would be viewed as cruel and inhuman treatment!

Too often, a spouse elects to ignore the warning signs of trading up out of fear that she may discover something she does not want to know. Clients have told me that, especially in long- term relationships, that not knowing whether their spouse is having an affair is better than learning the truth. As one client revealed, "perhaps the woman in the seductive shoes will go away and our life can return to normal once again."

In many cases, the high-income achieving spouse may announce that he is unhappy in his relationship, has been unhappy for some time, and wants to separate. Though at first the other spouse may have been surprised by the revelation, had she recognized the early symptoms, she may have had the opportunity to save her marriage.

LARRY'S STORY

Larry had been married for almost thirty years and the best way to describe him would be to say he was definitely a "geek" in high school. His two children were both in college. He and his wife had always enjoyed a very nice lifestyle and as a couple appeared to be a perfect fit. He had started a software company in the nineties that he sold a few years ago to a publicly traded company. Almost overnight, he became a millionaire, as he was able to exercise his stock options. Though he continued to work as a consultant, work was no longer a 9 to 5 requirement. To occupy his spare time, he began attending art auctions as he was always fascinated by art. His wife had no interest in art and thought nothing of him attending the auctions at night. That is where he met his girlfriend. She was divorced, received a large settlement from her Ex, and had plenty of time to play! Larry's wife thought it was strange that he was suddenly interested in men's clothing as she always bought his clothes. He now did his own shopping with total disregard for the price of the item. When he began to wear cologne she questioned him. Finally, after six months of denying to his wife that something was wrong, he admitted to having an affair.

SPECIAL SITUATION—DOES HE THINK HE IS BETTER THAN YOU?

My husband and I divorced over religious differences. He thought he was God, and I didn't.

My wife is a wonderful cook and I am not just saying that because I have to live under the same roof as her. She has passion for cooking and enjoys pleasing others with her delectable offerings. As a result, even if I had the slightest desire to attempt making egg salad, our kitchen is off limits to me. Likewise, I graciously accept this rule. Furthermore, I am proud to tell the world what a great cook my wife is.

Compare this with the spouse who is always telling the world how great he is and how inferior his spouse is. Note, we are not talking about so called stereotypes such as that men are better at reading maps or women are neater. Instead, the following story was told by a client about her constantly bragging husband.

MARY'S STORY

Mary married her first husband shortly after they both graduated college. Within less than a year, they both realized they were too young for such a commitment and parted amicably.

Five years later, and with her doctorate diploma in psychology on her office wall, she was ready to get serious about meeting someone again. Enter Paul. He too had a brief marriage and was looking to remarry.

Like most new relationships, things were great; he sent her flowers and was very complimentary. But Paul had an "edge" to him in that he relished in telling people how wonderful he was. At the same time, he never hesitated to tell the free world of his wife's shortcomings. At first, Mary took these comments in stride. But, in time, it became a great source of irritation especially when he "put her down" in public. Though she would tell him how hurtful these remarks were, it did not seem to matter as the very next opportunity Paul had to humiliate Mary, he would.

Finally, at a birthday party for her best friend, Mary left in tears after he proceeded to tell the room how horrible she was in the kitchen and made some lewd remarks referring to her as a "cold fish" in the sack.

He can dish it out but how much can you take? Do any of the following apply to your relationship? If they do, don't fool yourself that he will change or that you will get use to it. You won't.

- He tells you he is better looking than you
- He says he is smarter than you
- He embarrasses you in front of your friends
- He makes you feel inferior
- He makes hurtful comments about your lack of knowledge
- He is conceited
- He does not accept fault
- He does not accept failure
- He claims to be a perfectionist
- He says if you have children they will get their brains from him
- He refers to your siblings and/ or your parents as being uneducated or not worldly enough, or worse

BLENDED FAMILIES AND
THE BRADY BUNCH NIGHTMARE

The song, **Love and Marriage,** includes the lyrics:

> *"Love and marriage, love and marriage*
> *Goes together like a horse and carriage*
> *This I tell you brother*
> *You can't have one without the other"*

If you have kids from a prior marriage, they are the carriage and an integral part for there to be love and marriage. Accordingly, before you say I do again, consider the following:

He's wonderful, has a fantastic job with a great future. But he was married before and has no children. You are also divorced and raising your two children. As much as he loves you and you love him, what happens if your children do not share that love for your future spouse? Being older, wiser, and possibly better funded won't wipe out complications. Yes, Cupid has struck. Yes, you feel young again. Just remember you're not a kid anymore. You have children now.

☙ BEFORE YOU BECOME A BLENDED FAMILY

If you are like the majority of couples facing remarriage, one or both of you have children from your previous marriage. As such, this creates unique challenges separate and apart from all of the issues concerning remarriage.

FACTOID: 65 percent of all remarriages include children from a previous marriage.

When a man marries a woman with children from a previous marriage, she is sometimes unkindly referred to as "having a lot of baggage." I hate that phrase as it paints a picture of a marriage doomed from the start. As such, one of the challenges is to make sure that the marriage gets off to a good start. Planning occurs long before saying I do, again.

To do so, it is important to involve your children once your relationship turns to the discussion of marriage. This is not to imply that your children need to meet and screen every person you date. They should not be surprised one day by hearing your announcement that you are getting married again.

Whether you have primary custody, split custody or visitation of your children, accepting a step- parent into their life is just as much an adjustment for them as it is for you as your remarriage will change both your life and theirs. As you can appreciate, your children have already experienced the breakup of their parents which was probably something they did not want. Therefore, including your children rather than shielding them from that new special person will help in getting your marriage off to a good start.

Likewise, be prepared to answer your children's questions so that they do not spend sleepless nights worrying about the answers. Depending on their age, common questions children will ask include:

- Will we have to move?
- Where are we going to live?
- Will I have the same friends?
- Will I still see my Dad or Mom?
- Do I have to call him Dad?

♛ HOW DOES HE REALLY FEEL ABOUT YOUR KIDS?

"Whenever I date a guy I think, 'Is this the man I want my children to spend their weekends with?'" — Rita Rudner

Before you say I do, again, consider the person you are marrying as he not only will become your spouse but also the step-parent of your children.

The following is a checklist of questions to ask your fiancé about his feelings toward your children.

CHAPTER TWENTY-THREE

- What concerns do you have about my children?
- What role do you see yourself playing in raising my children?
- How do you handle discipline?
- If I need your help, how flexible are you at rearranging your schedule?
- Will you be jealous when I spend time with my children?
- How do you feel about your/our money going to pay for the needs of my children?

This last question should be asked very delicately as whether or not you are receiving support, there will always be times when you will incur expenses for your children that may not be fully covered by the support you receive. Though you may be getting a monthly check for support, I have never had a client who can account for how that support check is applied. If finances are of major concern, his answer to this question may provide a window as to what life for you and the kids might be like if you say I do, again.

Likewise, if he has children, you may have your own concerns. Consider asking the following questions of him:

- What concerns do you have about your children having a stepparent?
- What role do you see me in raising your children?
- How do you handle disciplining your children?
- How do you feel about me disciplining your children?
- Have your children expressed their feelings about me/us?
- How is your relationship with your former spouse?

PRACTICAL POINT! You should never marry someone only because you see that person's checkbook as a way of having more money for you and your children. See Chapter Eight for a further discussion.

MY CHILDREN COME FIRST!

Both of you had lives before you met. You each took different paths that eventually led to finding each other. Along the way, one or both of you may have had children. When entering a second marriage, all of the pieces have to neatly fit. If not, you will never find happiness.

Often, one of the greatest obstacles to achieving marital bliss is accepting that the child of the person you are about to marry has a permanent place in your husband's life that was established long before there was you.

You cannot compete for that love or think you should be able to. If you and your intended cannot strike a balance, you need to walk away.

Likewise, when there is a child from a previous relationship, your future spouse must make room in his life for your needs and wants and must respect you just as you must respect him. If he is not willing to do so, the marriage is doomed. Regardless of how great things are when the two of you are alone, you will always feel you are being passed over for the sake of his child unless you gain his respect. This is not to say that he must always yield to your needs or wants. Instead, everyone has to find their place.

JOEL'S STORY

Joe had never married and was approaching forty. Sheila had a child from a previous marriage. She was still bitter about her divorce though the marriage had ended over three years ago. Sheila's daughter Stacy was a bright, pretty girl. Like any teenager, she often expressed her independence which Joel viewed as disrespect for her mother. Specifically, Stacy would talk back to Sheila and downright rude to her. Whenever Joel brought Stacy's conduct up to Sheila, she defended Stacy saying that she "comes from a broken home."

Joel was very tolerant and knew it was not his place to try to resolve any matter directly. But he could not ignore reacting when Stacy stormed out of the house shouting obscenities when Sheila refused to let her go to a concert. Joel and Sheila began to quarrel. But instead of listening to Joel, Sheila said that Stacy will always come first and "that is the way it is, take it or leave it." After a few weeks, Joel took her up on her offer and ended the relationship.

THE JEANS STILL FIT BUT
I'VE GROWN TIRED OF THEM

Marriage is a lifetime commitment. Unlike the jeans in your closet that are no longer stylish, remarriage is not something that if you get tired of, no longer like, or just doesn't excite you, you simply throw away. So before you say I do again, consider the following. If not, you will grow complacent but not happy.

♛ BOREDOM IS LIKE A SLOW DEATH THAT WILL KILL A MARRIAGE

In choosing your partner the second time around, consider whether he is more exciting or boring. If it is the latter, you may well resign yourself to the fact that your life could be no different than that of your pet. That is, each day when you fill your kitty's bowl with the same cat food that was poured in yesterday, that very well could be your life. No excitement. No variety. No change. Though it is said that opposites attract, it is because most of us like change. Why else would we wear different clothes each day, grow a mustache or change a hair style, and dine at different restaurants. It is because we want to experience change and don't thrive on boredom.

SHELLY'S STORY

Shelly had been divorced only two years when she met Steve through an online dating service. From their first date, there was chemistry. Within a few dates, they became exclusive and on New Year's Eve, he proposed.

As Shelly related, their sex life was okay while dating but Steve was not passionate when they made love. He was more interested in getting to the finish line and wasn't always a team player. However, he had so many other great qualities and he absolutely adored her children.

By year five of their marriage, sex had been reduced to Saturday nights as Steve said, he was always too tired from work to have sex during the week. He also had a code phrase for when he wanted to have sex. His line was, "Do you want to go into the Jacuzzi?" So, being the good wife that she was, Shelly performed her wifely duties though it was never performed in the hot tub which she thought could be exciting.

That next summer, when Shelly's Ex had the children for two weeks, she decided it was time to spice things up in the bedroom. One day after Steve left for work, she went to Victoria's Secret and bought some sexy lingerie. She also called Steve at work and told him that she was making a romantic dinner and that she "was serving dessert in the Jacuzzi." When Steve entered the home, the table was beautifully set with candles and rose petals. Shelly was standing by the oven wearing a sheer, sexy nighty and holding two glasses of wine. Without noticing her efforts, he put down his briefcase, took a seat at the table and asked, "What's for dinner?" They had a nice meal followed by sex in the bedroom which was a rarity for Steve since it was a weeknight. However, never once did he compliment Shelly or even say anything about the sexy outfit. She decided the next day that she needed more excitement in her life and filed for divorce.

LEGALLY SPEAKING! Boredom is a silent killer of marriage. Though it probably does not rank as high as someone cheating or having an abusive or addictive personality, it is still just as lethal. The problem with boredom is that it is often more tolerable and marriages go on longer only because a spouse will overlook it and find other positive aspects of the marriage to rationalize that this is something "we should try to work out." However, like a slow growing disease, unless aggressive steps are taken, boredom will almost always prove fatal to marital harmony.

MARY'S STORY
"HE LIKED TO EAT AT "SIZZLER" BUT THERE WAS NO SIZZLE IN THEIR MARRIAGE!"

Mary was married only three years to Stewart. It was her second marriage but he was never married before. They had no children and both enjoyed their work. But on weekends, Mary was looking for some excitement. While she had to make all the plans, Stewart was content to be sitting in front of his TV. Whenever she asked Stewart where he would like to eat, his answer was always Sizzler. When I asked her why Sizzler, she replied it was because she could have a salad and Stewart was able to order his steak and potatoes. He never deviated and would bark at her if she suggested somewhere else to dine. Even when they went out with friends, his eyes would always point to the steak entrée.

For the first year of marriage, she did not let it bother her. She rationalized that Stewart's mother did a terrible job by not exposing him to other foods. She told him that he was missing out on life by ordering the same old boring meal every time. By the second year, she became more assertive and told him that she wished he would take charge of making plans and not always leave everything up to her. Mary told him that she was bored.

Eventually, the parties acted like roommates and not husband and wife; Mary did her own thing on weekends while Stewart sat at home. Come Saturday night, she would rent a video and they both stared at the screen. Their interest in sex became nonexistent. Finally, Mary made weekend plans for her and Stewart to go to Las Vegas for one last chance to get their marriage back on track. But on the drive home she knew she had to make a choice; either stay with a man who chose to eat Alpo everyday or move on. The choice was clear.

I don't particularly like Sushi. It's okay, but I limit my Sushi intake to California Rolls as there is just something about eating raw fish that goes against my grain. But I do like Chinese and Italian food. In fact, I can't really say there is any kind of ethnic food that I don't like. That doesn't mean I would want to sit down to a bowl of pasta or a plate of Chicken Chow Mien every night!

REMARRYING FOR THE LONG RUN

Have you ever done something and wondered the next day what were you thinking? Hopefully, your new relationship is not that fragile. However, before you say I do again, you must consider if your intended to be has those qualities that you want for the long run. Consider the following:

♛ CAN A PERSON BE TOO NICE?

Just like opposites attract, too often we are drawn to someone with a similar personality that we knew from a previous relationship. Perhaps since we know what to expect, there will not be any surprises. But just because you are not traveling through chartered waters does not also guarantee that the seas will be calm.

When analyzing what went wrong with a prior marriage, we tend to overlook complacency. Oftentimes it is the things that do not set off alarms that go under the radar screen for a long period of time. Then one day you realize things are not right but can't pinpoint exactly what it is that is causing the marriage not to work. After the marriage has ended, and you have had time to look back, you find it extremely annoying. Therefore, you need to proceed cautiously with any new relationship so that the subtle behavior is not out there lurking and hidden from plain view.

JOLENE'S STORY
"SHE WANTED A 'MANLY' MAN"

Jolene was one of five girls. She described her father as a big, burly guy who had a larger bark than bite. She always felt safe when he was around. When she married Bill her friends were surprised. Bill was short, kind of scrawny, and nothing like the other guys she dated. But she said he was one of the sweetest guys she ever knew. He was attentive, a good listener, patient, and sensitive. They never fought and he always agreed with her decisions. Sounds too good to be true, right? But this personality was what eventually caused trouble in their marriage.

When Jolene consulted with our office, she told stories of how this sweet and sensitive guy was also meek and timid. She said Bill did everything for her but was also afraid of his own shadow. He could not defend himself or her. One time at the movies, a person sitting in front of them would not stop talking. She asked her husband to tell him to stop. He did not respond. The talking continued and Bill did nothing. This annoyed

Jolene more than the man talking. After Jolene and Bill left the movie they fought about this but it was never resolved. There were many similar incidents that she related.

When I asked her if this was enough to throw away her marriage, Jolene said she couldn't have respect for someone who did not have respect for himself. She also could not see herself continuing to live with such a weak individual.

How often have you heard it said that girls want to marry someone like their Dad? Well, presuming Dad is not some sexual deviant, men and women often look for attributes they saw in their parents when choosing a spouse. In Jolene's case, Bill was nothing like her father but is this enough of a reason to end a marriage? At first glance, one might conclude that Jolene was a shallow person. She was willing to take off her wedding ring only because she wasn't married to some macho guy who enjoyed stepping all over people. But it would seem difficult to remain in a relationship if you cannot respect the person you are married to.

♛ IS YOUR FUTURE PARTNER CHALLENGED?

In high school, a lot of my friends bragged that when they graduated college, there was a job waiting for them in their fathers' business. In addition, there would be a nice starting salary and they would eventually own the business.

My Dad did not have a business I could inherit. Though I wanted from the time I was a little boy to go to law school, I did think how cool it was that my friends would never have to compete for a job. In a sense, from the time they were young, they were fed with a silver spoon.

When I went to my twentieth high school reunion, I caught up with many of the guys from high school. To my surprise, though they did go to work for their Dads, almost all of them had married and divorced. Only years later did I make a connection between business complacency and failed marriages. When something is given to you, you lose your competitive edge. This loss sometimes spills over on how you look at marriage. A spouse wants someone who is strong, has convictions and opinions. That doesn't mean you want to be with someone who is going to argue with you on whether it is partly cloudy or partly sunny today. Likewise, marriage thrives on change and dies without a constant supply of energy.

The following is my predictor of whether your life with your fiancé will be same old/same old or full of excitement. Of course this is not scientific and I have no statistics to back me up. But when you read the list, consider whether the person you are now with falls into any of these categories. If he does, and you need more, now may be the right time to change directions.

✓ Is he stuck on one idea and can't move forward?
✓ Is he unhappy or unwilling to consider change?
✓ Is he not willing to try new things?
✓ Is he stubborn or too agreeable?
✓ Is he a dreamer but not a thinker?
✓ Is he not easily challenged?
✓ Does he see his future as something he has no control over
✓ Is he always part of the background and never takes center stage?
✓ Does he have low energy and always tired
✓ Does he pass on taking on anything that requires making a decision?

♛ YOU THINK YOU HAVE FOUND "THE ONE"

"He has a job, owns his own car, and doesn't live with his mother. I think he's the one!"

The above statement is written as a lark. But who is "the one?" Is he the person who makes your heart go "pitter patter?" Is he the one you most want to share that morning cup of coffee with? Or is he the one who is going to erase all of the misery that you have lived through from your first divorce and give you a fairy tale future?

Perhaps he is all these things and more. But often when someone says they have found "the one," their search may not have been very extensive and have instead found the wrong one!

PERSONALITIES THAT SEEM SO RIGHT BUT MAY BE SO WRONG!

Many of my clients from failed second marriages thought they had found "the one." Surprisingly, they met this person within a short period of time after the first divorce was finalized. While the parties shared so much in common, what would later prove not to work was overshadowed by the excitement of meeting someone new.

Before you say I do again, have you said any of the following about your fiancé?

- He finishes my sentence with what I was going to say
- He could be my twin
- We share the exact same interests
- He understands me better than I understand myself

Just because you are divorced, you are not on a mission to find Mr. Right. Therefore take your time. Otherwise, you may instead end up with Mr. Right now.

♕ I'M A LITTLE BIT COUNTRY—HE'S A LITTLE BIT ROCK N' ROLL (DO OPPOSITES REALLY ATTRACT?)

For those of you old enough to remember, Donny and Marie Osmond had a hit song in the 70's that was popularized on their television show. The point of the song was that, as brother and sister, they shared many differences but always got along.

When choosing a spouse, we often broadcast to our friends that

"Joe and I have nothing in common but that's what makes it so great," or

"She's interested in everything I do."

As you consider remarriage, you may find that opposites do not necessarily attract. And differences in opinions, values, and religious beliefs will cause stress in the marriage that if not resolved early on could lead to the breakdown of the marriage.

Accordingly, before you say I do again, take inventory of that person and his or her beliefs. The following are some questions to ponder:

- Do you consider yourself liberal or conservative?
- Are you registered to vote?
- Do you vote?
- What is your opinion about legalized abortion?
- What is your opinion about teaching religion in school?
- Do you consider yourself a religious person/do you practice a religion?
- Are you charitable?
- Do you ever volunteer?

🌱FAMILY VALUES

If you are close to your family, you will always be in conflict with your spouse if he or she does not share the same values. Whether it is getting together for Thanksgiving, opening presents on Christmas morning, or any other family event, in time you will start to resent your spouse if you find yourself attending these occasions by yourself.

In getting ready for before you say I do, again, it is important to question how your fiancé shares your same family values. If his responses do not pass your test, STOP, and change directions.

DENISE'S STORY

Denise had two older brothers and her parents had a long-term marriage. She ranked the love of her family on the top of her list for what she valued most. Derek's parents were divorced and he spend much of his childhood years being raised by his mother and spending a few weeks each summer with his Dad.

When Denise and Derek discussed getting married, they talked about everything except family. During the first year of their marriage, the calendar was filled with family birthdays and anniversaries as well as holiday gatherings. When Denise and Derek's first anniversary was approaching, her Mom suggested a family barbeque. Besides, there was that part of the wedding cake that was still sitting and taking up space in her freezer.

When she told Derek, he balked at the idea saying he had already attended too many family events and that he "wasn't going." Though he did oblige to attend, they fought bitterly that night after they got home and the fighting escalated from then on. Finally, after only six more months, his verbal abuse that resulted any time Denise would mention her family led to Denise leaving.

SPECIAL SITUATION: RELIGION AND REMARRIAGE

Discussions about religion can be rather uncomfortable. Perhaps it is because religion is looked upon as something private. Or maybe because the excitement of love is so great that you do not want to run the chance of ruining what you have.

Regardless, if you have strong religious convictions, the time to find out whether your partner is going to share these same values is long before you say I do, again.

WENDY'S STORY

Wendy was married to Gary for twenty years when they divorced after she found out he was cheating on her. They were both raised Jewish and practiced their faith during their marriage which included the Bar Mitzvah of her two children. Two years after her divorce, and approaching her fiftieth birthday, she met Evan. He too was divorced with grown sons.

During their one year courtship, the issue of religion came up only twice. The first time was when she invited Evan to her brother's house for a Passover Seder to which he politely declined. The second time was when they planned their wedding ceremony and Evan said that he preferred a nondenominational minister to marry them which she agreed to.

They were married in September in a small ceremony with just immediate family and their closest friends in attendence. A few weeks later it was the Jewish New Year. Wendy did not expect Evan to accompany her to temple but was hurt when he said he was surprised that she would lose a day of work to go to temple. However, she did not discuss the matter with him.

The holiday of Chanukah was in late December and Wendy told Evan that it was her family tradition to have a Chanukah party. The weekend before, she began decorating her home with the many stored boxes filled with Chanukah ornaments. Evan, however, did not help her and stayed in another room.

Finally, sensing her resentment, she confronted him which resulted in which he expressed his negative feelings toward all organized religion and that he would not partake in any party. She felt foolish when she asked him why he never expressed his feelings before and he answered that he didn't think it mattered that much.

The Chanukah party took place without Evan and he never saw Wendy's family again. Soon after the holidays, Wendy filed for divorce.

If religion is an important issue for you, part of planning for remarriage includes having a discussion about his religious beliefs. The following are suggested questions to ask:

- Were you raised with a religious belief?
- Do you now practice your religion by worshipping on a regular basis?
- Do you follow religious traditions?
- (If your faith is different from his) Is it a problem for you that my religion is different from yours?

- Will you expect me to participate in your religious traditions?
- Will you participate in my religious traditions?
- What role should religion play in our wedding ceremony?
- (If you are planning on having children together) What religion would you want to raise our children?
- (If he was married before) Was religion in issue in your past marriage?
- Have your parents/siblings expressed any feelings or concerns to you that we are of different faiths? How have you responded to their feelings or concerns?

If you and your fiancé have strong religious differences, the answer that he provides may be a deal breaker for the marriage going forward. In addition, always remember that not only are you marrying the person standing at the altar, you are also marrying into his family. Consider the following:

RENE'S STORY

Rene was raised Catholic and her parents were deeply upset when she divorced. They did not believe in divorce and repeatedly had told her to "work things out at least for the sake of her children."

After a few years of living single, Rene met Eraj and they began dating. Eraj was born in Iran, raised in the United States, and was a Muslim. When Rene's parents met Eraj, they immediately expressed their dislike for him. When Rene told her parents that she was thinking of remarriage, they threatened to cut her off from her future inheritance if she went through with the marriage. She did marry Eraj but lost her relationship with her parents.

In Rene's case, she had to make a terrible decision between her parents and the man she loved.

LEGALLY SPEAKING! One's misrepresentations about their religious beliefs may be grounds for annulment. As a result, a court that finds the marriage contract was based on fraud will sever the contract and the parties will be restored to their unmarried status as if the marriage ceremony never occurred. The bottom line is that you can legally say you were never married before!

SEVEN COMMANDMENTS BEFORE YOU SAY "I DO, AGAIN

1. Do not marry someone who has characteristics of your Ex that you resented or are offensive to you. If he smokes, he is not going to stop just because you want him to.

2. Do not plan to change the person you are marrying? It won't happen! If he doesn't like to shave on weekends, live with it, or don't get married.

3. Do not marry out of impulse. Impulse buying is picking up a magazine at the checkout counter where you buy your groceries. Instead check out from head to toe and inside and out before you say I do, again.

4. If your religion and beliefs are important to you, do not expect someone to adopt your convictions.

5. Make sure it is love and not companionship. If you don't want to be alone, consider adopting a dog. Fido will give you unconditional love which no marriage can offer.

6. Make sure you are truly in love and not simply in love with the title.

7. Enter remarriage with the idea that it will work and that divorce is not an easy "go to" option if it doesn't.

And What About . . . ?

Is there a big age difference between you and your fiancé? Is he a widower? Are you thinking of remarrying your Ex? The following chapter discusses these and other unique situations, and are presented to make your next trip down the aisle, your last trip to the altar.

❦ MARRYING TOO YOUNG

Are you too young to get married again? Is your spouse-to-be, even if he or she has never been married, too young to say I do?

For a first marriage, planning a wedding and taking a honeymoon is probably one of the most exciting events one can experience in a lifetime. The world is your stage and you have your entire future to enjoy life as husband and wife. What could be better?

> PRACTICAL POINT: For some, the question as to when is the right time to marry is based on age. For others, if he or she is not mature enough to take on the responsibilities of marriage, there is never the right age.

For many young couples who walk down the aisle, their lives begin and continue as a fairy tale relationship. She has met her knight in shining armor and she is all he could ever dream of. They rent their first apartment, he gets a promotion, save up for the down payment on their first home, start their family, and live happily ever after.

But for some, the fairy tale has an unhappy ending. Sometime during the first few years of marriage, one or both spouses starts to ponder the question what did the man in the black robe mean when he asked, "Do you take this person to be your lawful wedded wife until death do you part?" Does that mean I cannot get a drink with my friends after work? Or have I agreed to trade Friday night at the club for Friday night at the Laundromat?

No matter how passionate a relationship may be in the beginning, the honeymoon does not last forever. Not to mention the added stress created by work and paying bills tests any relationship regardless of your age. But for those who marry young, some feel they may have sacrificed experiencing life for the commitment of marriage. And just because you are chronologically older the second time around, it does necessarily mean you are also wiser. Likewise, your future spouse may also be immature and not ready to walk down the aisle.

The first sign that the marriage may be in trouble is when one starts to rethink the commitment. Usually, a spouse does not verbalize his or her feelings with his partner though the feelings may be shared with best friends. For men, the husband may feel envy about the guy at work who boasts every Monday morning about his latest sexual conquest. For women, she is flattered by a male coworker whose actions she interprets as flirtatious. Whether they are or are not is irrelevant. What matters is she is excited that another male finds her attractive.

JOHN AND SUE'S STORY

John and Sue came into our office for a consultation and told me they met in high school, began dating in their senior year, and were married a month after graduating college. Now, three years later, John and Sue were renting an apartment, making a car payment, and were saddled with credit card debts. At age twenty-five, many of John's friends were still single and he expressed he thought he was missing something but could not put into words what that "something" was.

They both said there was no animosity between them; Sue said she still loved John, but did not want him to be unhappy for the rest of his life. Accordingly, she did want to stand in the way of his happiness though she wanted to keep trying to stay together.

At this point it was my professional opinion this was not a couple ready to proceed with a divorce. And as I often do, I gave them some nonlegal advice to go away to some place special for a weekend, away from phone calls and other interruptions to see if there is still that chemistry that first brought them together. Not surprisingly, his Mother had already given him the same advice. The best part was he did not have to pay her a consultation fee.

♛ THE AGE EQUATION—MARRYING THE MUCH OLDER SPOUSE

How old is too old of an age difference to get remarried? If you ask movie star Demi Moore who is fifteen years older than Ashton Kutcher, she would say that age does not matter. She already had three kids when she met Ashton. Actress Mary Tyler Moore would probably answer the same as she is eighteen years older than husband Dr. Robert Levine.

Even though my wine connoisseur friends tell me that a fine wine ages with time, this comparison does not always apply to other palatable treats. For example, bread left out too long gets stale and moldy and a sliced apple turns brown. It would be terribly unfair to stereotype all older persons as not being as desirable as a new, young wine. When contemplating marriage the second time around, a large age difference between you and your intended may become an even larger factor in the future.

PRACTICAL POINT! Thanks to advances in Science, the average life span of a male in the United States has risen to seventy-nine years and for females it is more than eighty. It is true that we are more active than our parents and more educated about what we should eat. But just because AARP has promoted the phrase that "today's 50 is yesterday's 30," that does not mean that fifty-year-old today might not be in diapers tomorrow!

MARILYN'S STORY

Marilyn raised two children with her first husband Bill and admits she would have divorced him sooner but for the sake of the children held on for as long as she could. Once the kids were off to college, Marilyn decided that she wanted more out of life than her husband could provide. She admits that she was selfish by wanting the finer things such as going to expensive restaurants and taking luxury vacations.

In her pursuit of "champagne wishes and caviar dreams," she met Donald online. Chatting quickly turned to talking and finally meeting. After a series of dates that began in very fine restaurants and often ended with dessert and more in Donald's penthouse condominium, Marilyn decided she was going to ask Bill for a divorce.

Bill was not surprised at Marilyn's announcement as he suspected something was going on. What did surprise him, as well as all of Marilyn's friends and her two sons, was the fact that Donald was planning his sixty-fifth birthday which made him an even twenty years older than Marilyn!

The two continued dating and a year later they were married with Donald surprising his young bride with a month long honeymoon in the Greek islands. The first five years of marriage seemed wonderful as Marilyn enjoyed every opulence she forever dreamed of. But shortly after the sixth year, Donald fell and broke his hip. At seventy-one, he was not as spry as he used to be and the recovery took a lot longer than had he been in his fifties. Prostate problems soon followed and walking became difficult for Donald due to his badly arthritic knees. As a result, Donald much preferred Marilyn cooking dinner or ordering in rather than having to struggle to leave his home.

With boredom having replaced excitement, Marilyn filed for divorce. Fortunately for her, she had not signed a prenuptial agreement (as discussed in Chapter Sixteen) and received a generous settlement which allowed her plenty of money to dine forever in fine restaurants, alone!

PRACTICAL POINT: Most young women who are attracted to older men seek surrogate father figures, maturity to balance their own insecurity, or someone with the means and inclination to be a "sugar daddy." Many marriages between a younger woman and older man are loving and successful. However, couples with a twenty to twenty-five year age gap are a rarity as it is difficult to sustain a long-term relationship when each party's goals are different. The younger woman may expect to complete her education, solidify her ambitions, build a career, and eventually raise a family. The older man is no longer interested in investing time and energy into building his life; he's already done so and now wants to reap what he has sown. If he does want a family, he surely won't want to delay fatherhood.

CELEBRITY HAPPILY EVER AFTER REMARRIAGES?

The following celebrity couples have two things in common; they all have been married before and enjoy large age differences between them.

- Warren Beatty and Annette Bening-Annette is 21 years younger
- Clint Eastwood is 25 years older than his wife Dina.
- Michael Douglas is 25 years older than Catherine Zeta-Jones
- Soon-Yi is 35 years younger than Woody Allen
- Francesa Annis and Ralph Fiennes-Ralph is 19 years younger
- Mary Tyler Moore and Dr. Robert Levine. Robert is 18 years younger
- Jerry Seinfeld and Jessica. Jessica is 18 years younger
- Demi Moore and Ashton Kutcher- Demi Moore was 42, and Ashton Kutcher was 27 when they wed—a 15 year difference
- Martha Raye married Mark Harris who was 33 years younger
- Geena Davis and Dr. Reza Jarrahy. Reza is 15 years younger
- Tony Bennett and Susan Crow. Tony is about 33 years older than Susan
- Julianne Moore and Bart Freundlich. Bart is 9 years younger
- Tony Randall and Heather Harlan Heather was 50 years younger

♛ I WANT A BABY

Did you divorce your first spouse because you could not conceive? This may not have been the sole reason your marriage failed. Most couples enter into a marriage thinking that someday they will have a family. I remember when my wife was pregnant with our first child, she would fantasize of the day we would walk our little girl down the aisle. And I thought about the baseball games I would attend with my son.

We have been blessed with both a son and daughter who every day has brought indefinable pleasure to our lives. Other married couples are not always as fortunate. The inability to have a family often strains a marriage. Consider the following:

JEFF AND ASHLEY'S STORY

Jeff and Ashley were in their late twenties when they married. They both came from large families and family events were a big part of their lives.

After a few years of marriage, they began trying to start a family. However, after two years of trying, they were not successful and began investigating whether there was a medical reason why they could not conceive. But test after test after test, the results were inconclusive. So, with no medical reason, there was some initial optimism in the belief that if they kept trying, it was going to happen.

Then Ashley got a hold of a Self-help book, which explained that they were trying too hard and needed to relax. Ashley's girlfriends offered her unsolicited, nonmedical advice, which only added to her frustration. Jeff was totally opposed to the idea of adoption.

To make matters worse, friends all around them had children while their parents and other relatives kept pestering them about when were they going to start a family. It seemed like every weekend they were invited to a baby's christening or another birthday party. Though they put forth their best face possible, the frustration they shared started to show.

Finally, Ashley and Jeff started to grow apart with Ashley wrongfully accepting full responsibility and labeling herself a failure. Tensions continued to mount and many nights they retired to bed in a fight which continued to fester as the week went on. Finally, Jeff announced that he had been unhappy and wanted to separate.

Ashley's desire to become a Mom overshadowed the relationship that she had with Jeff and eventually led to the demise of their marriage. But what if one partner wants children and the other does not?

If procreation is the primary reason for marriage, it is only logical that you would not stay in a relationship if you cannot have children. But before you say I do again, you must analyze how important having children is to both of you.

Accordingly, before you say I do, again, if having children is part of your marriage equation, you must have a dialogue with your fiancé before you walk down the aisle as this is not one of those subjects that would be better off discussed later than now. If you and he are not in total agreement about having children as well as the timetable for when you would like to begin a family, don't go any further. If one of you wants kids and the other does not, it is a deal breaker.

♛ MARRYING A WIDOW(ER)

When one marries someone who has lost a first spouse, there are additional issues that must be addressed before you or he says I do, again.

Understanding your fiancé's grief

Earlier in this book I refer to the often used phrase

"Time is the greatest healer."

Regardless of how much time has passed since the loss of a loved one, the grieving goes on though it may not be as evident. Therefore, do not ignore or run away from your fiancé's grief. Instead, it is better to talk openly and honestly about it.

You cannot replace the loss of a loved one

Your relationship is new and separate from the marriage your fiancé had with his or her loved one. Likewise, do not go into the marriage with the expectation that you can replace the love that your fiancé had with his or her spouse.

Don't let material possessions pull you apart

Your fiancé had a life with his or her spouse before you that has now been taken away. As a result, there may be picture albums, photos on the wall, and other visual memories of the late spouse. Accept there was this life before and try to find ways of compromising. Have discussions as to what possessions should be kept and which should be stored or given away. Regardless, never make decisions for your fiancé as to the disposition of these possessions. Instead show respect for them.

Respect other family members' time to mourn

While his family may or may not immediately accept you into the new extended family fold, remember that they have experienced a great loss and are dealing with the backlash of grief. They may fear that their daughter's/sister's memory will fade into obscurity just because your husband decided to remarry, and may subconsciously blame you for this. If you remain constantly focused on their bereavement, it will become much easier for you to deal with any negativity on their part. As with anyone who has suffered the loss of a loved one to death, allow them their memories and be patient as they learn to grow to love who you are and respect your place in your husband's life.

Never compare yourself with the late spouse

You will not score any points with your fiancé by trying to compare yourself with the late spouse. There is no competition and it does not matter whether you are a better cook and that the Ex could not boil water. The two of you are together not because you are a clone of the late spouse. Instead, the two of you have your own unique bond and that cannot be duplicated. Likewise, never feel insecure that he or she is comparing you to the late spouse. Perhaps it is that difference that made you so appealing.

Expect that there will be periods of grief and learn how to handle them

The calendar is a reminder of events; anniversaries, birthdays, special occasions, and yes, even the day someone died. It would be foolish to assume that your fiancé will not be reminded of these events on that particular day. Accordingly, expect that he or she may express grief or act in a manner where he or she is covering up feelings of grief so as to shield you from such feelings. Approach such calendar anniversaries with honesty. Do not limit communication and instead be a sensitive listener.

♛ IS IT YOU HE LUSTS OR YOUR BANK ACCOUNT THAT HE WANTS TO MAKE LOVE TO?

Though not everyone wins the lottery like Heather Mills did in her divorce from the Beatles' Paul McCartney, with inflated real estate prices, a sale of a business, or hitting payday on the stock, it is not so unusual to receive a divorce settlement that leaves you on easy street.

If you are fortunate enough to be left financially comfortable for the rest of your life, be weary of suitors who want to share your wealth. Just like persons who win the lottery, your name will be fair game as divorce proceedings are after all public record. Though the exact terms of a settlement are not always disclosed, it does not take a sophisticated divorce predator a long time to figure out who you are.

Note, men who prey on wealthy divorcees come in all shapes and sizes and can be easily disguised. Often, it is only after they have caused you financial harm that their true identity is revealed.

EVE'S STORY

Eve was married to Brian who started a software company. The company had just received an offer to be purchased by a publicly traded conglomerate which would result in Brian receiving money and stock in an amount that would normally only be seen playing Monopoly. While Brian was developing software, he was also developing an amorous relationship with his secretary.

Eve had her suspicions and hired a private investigator. When she confronted Brian, he fessed up. Refusing to allow him to atone for his sins, she filed for divorce. And though California is a community property state where typically assets are split 50-50, Brian did not want to risk the public exposure that he felt could hurt the sale of his company going forward. Instead, he made Eve a very generous offer.

Within six months of her divorce, and having received her settlement, she spent her days contemplating how to invest her money. That's when she met Ryan. They were both attending an investment workshop. At the time, she did not know that while she was looking for worthwhile investments, he was trolling for an investor.

During a morning break, Ryan introduced himself to Eve and continued with every possible compliment he could offer. By the afternoon break, he had asked her out to dinner the next night. Within two weeks, he had showered Eve with flowers, fine wine, and romantic dinners.

By the end of the second week Eve was starstruck by Ryan. She admits that she became hypnotized by his big brown eyes and revealed to him everything that was private about her. And Ryan, being so calculated and good at his job, slowly drew Eve into his web as he began to tell her about his huge real estate deal that was about to close but was hung up by some financing issue. Giving only enough information about his "deal" which begged Eve to ask for more, she voluntarily offered to help him out anyway she could. Less than a week later, Ryan had vanished forever from Eve's life after cashing her check for $75,000.

PRACTICAL POINT: The period immediately following a divorce is when you are most vulnerable. Perhaps it is because you feel you need to make a right out of a wrong that you may do something out of character. Accordingly, before acting impulsively or without logic, pause and reconsider the situation. In most cases, your caution will be rewarded.

LEGALLY SPEAKING! Regardless of any financial settlement resulting from a divorce, a subsequent marriage will terminate the right to receive alimony. That is sometimes a mighty good reason to not say I do, again!

♕ IF YOU ARE A WIDOW—BE LEARY OF SUITORS

As discussed in Chapter Eleven, it is an extremely emotional time after the loss of a spouse as you are now suddenly alone. Though you may have the emotional support of your family and friends, when you put your head to your pillow at night and close your eyes, it can be a very frightening time adjusting to not having your loved one next to you.

For many persons who have experienced such a tragic loss, it is also a difficult time in their lives as you may have to rely on yourself to do things that you took for granted before or left to your spouse to do. Tasks as simple as taking out the trash cans or writing the checks to pay the bills may now be your responsibility. For some who are most vulnerable and susceptible to the prey of others, this time can be frightening. Consider the next story.

NAT'S STORY

Nat and Gloria were living in a retirement community enjoying their twilight years until she was diagnosed with stomach cancer. She died within six months. Becky was also a widow living on her late husband's social security check. Becky had also, as Nat's daughter often pointed out, "buried two previous husbands."

With a few days of his wife's funeral, Gloria became available offering to cook for Nat, and do his laundry. As Nat was financially comfortable, he returned the favor by taking her out to expensive restaurants, buying her groceries, and took her on a two week cruise through the Panama Canal. Nat's daughter kept warning her father that, "this woman was moving too fast" but he ignored her warnings as he said it was better than "being alone."

After less than a year since Gloria passed away, Nat and Becky decided to get married. Nat decided not to tell his daughter as he feared she would have stood up and objected. Instead, they were married in a Las Vegas Chapel. When he finally did give his daughter the news, she realized there was nothing she could do and rationalized that perhaps it was better for her father to have companionship rather than being alone.

Within a few months after he said "I do," he confided in his daughter that it was a mistake. Becky had sweet talked her way to being placed on his checking account. This allowed her to write checks to her grown children. She also enjoyed spending sprees at the mall where she treated herself to lavish clothing and jewelry and enjoyed using their credit cards to buy her grandchildren gifts.

♛ REMARRYING YOUR EX!

Do you miss the good times you had together?
Do you want to watch a rerun of the bad times?

After the tears of the divorce have dried up and you start dating again, it is not uncommon to come to the realization that the fish that are swimming in the pond are worst than your Ex was. Now that you have had time to think about it, he really wasn't that bad. Before you seriously consider saying I do again with your Ex, remember that a fine wine with proper care ages gracefully with time. Unfortunately, the same cannot always be said for men and women.

So why does your Ex look so good now? Before I answer, consider this analogy.

In my neighborhood, Mondays are trash days. On Sunday nights, I wheel out the cans filled with garbage that occasionally includes something that broke, no longer works, and cannot be fixed or costs too much to repair. By doing so, I have made a decision that we have no further use for this object. In comparison, wasn't your Ex that same person you wished to be hauled away with the rest of the garbage?

⚡ PRACTICAL POINT! If Mr. Ex was so Mr. Wrong, wouldn't your time be better spent looking for Mr. Right!

If your Ex is still in your life because of your children, or even casually, you may still have feelings for him. What you must resolve is whether these feelings are strong enough to try to make a go again at marriage.

KAREN'S STORY

Karen was married to Dennis for twenty-five years and had two grown sons when they divorced. Their separation was amicable and, in addition to issues concerning the boys, they did see each other at family events.

Eight years after their divorce was final, they were at a mutual friend's son's wedding. It was not awkward for them to be together as they had remained amicable. Well they started talking and Dennis even asked her to dance. Before the night was over, he suggested they have dinner together which Marilyn quickly accepted.

Over dinner, they discussed all of the relationships they had been in since the divorce. Both of them admitted they had not met anyone they wanted to become serious with. They also acknowledged how much they still had in common and decided to give it another try. They confessed they had seen other people but had never met the right person. Karen and Dennis married a year later and the second marriage lasted only long enough for them to file joint tax returns.

Though Karen and Dennis remembered the good times and how much they had in common, the passing of time allowed them to forget all the bad times that eventually caused their divorce. And, just like meeting an old friend or someone from high school that you have not seen for many years, there is a comfort level. Therefore, you don't have to keep the bathroom door closed unless you always did and you have already been intimate so there is nothing new.

Before you say I do, again with your Ex, take inventory of all the reasons that caused you to say I don't. Especially do not remarry your Ex because it is easier.

A CHECKLIST BEFORE REMARRYING YOUR EX:

In the movie business, it is more common for a sequel to not be as good as the original. In remarrying your Ex, the same often holds true. The following is a checklist before remarrying your Ex:

✓ Accept statistics that the cards are stacked against you. Remarriages to a former spouse have an even higher percentage of marriage failures.
✓ Make a list of everything that was right the first time around and compare it with a list of what was wrong. Weigh one list against the other.
✓ Analyze what caused the divorce. Was it money? A cheating spouse? An addictive behavior? There may have been many events that led up to it, but most of the time there is one dominant issue that was the catalyst.
✓ Remind yourself that though the day and month has changed, he may not have.
✓ Before moving ahead, resolve any unfinished issues. Perhaps she has never fessed up about her affair or he still has feelings for someone. Unresolved issues will only surface and show their ugly face at a later time if not resolved now.

✓ Getting back together in the best interest of your children is not always the best idea. In fact, it may be healthier for your children if the two of you stay apart!

✓ Consider marriage counseling to gain an objective opinion.

✓ Do not forget the past that caused your marriage to fail but build on it to make the remarriage a success.

✓ If before or after your separation, one or both of you were sarcastic toward the other, lose that tone. Communicate with positive expressions

✓ Talk to both sides' family members and friends to seek their opinion. They may have been reluctant to speak up the first time around but may be eager to talk now

PRACTICAL POINT: Proceed cautiously. You have already been to the altar, went on the honeymoon, and experienced life as husband and wife. He or she will still be there tomorrow if it was meant to be.

ELLEN'S STORY

Ellen and Bob were married for fifteen years but had no children. They had originally met in college and had a long history together. Their marriage was very volatile with Ellen finally leaving because she could no longer tolerate the verbal abuse. After the marriage ended, both parties dated other people but they still stayed in touch. They would occasionally get together for a drink and discussed their unsuccessful attempts to meet someone. After another year had passed, Bob suggested to Ellen that they should "give it another chance." He told her that he had matured and had even gone through an anger management course. She agreed to start dating Bob again but said she wanted to "take it slow." Within six months, they had moved in together and despite an outcry of opposition from her friends and family, they remarried.

However, before her diamond ring needed a cleaning, she realized that what she got the second time around was the same if not worse than the first time. Bob questioned every decision Ellen made and his verbal assaults sent her crying to bed every night. Six months later, she was in our office filing for a second divorce.

NEVER REMARRY ONLY FOR
THE SAKE OF YOUR CHILDREN!

It is not uncommon to hear that a couple stayed together for the sake of the children. As such, though the marriage was working, they accepted their commitment to be parents and placed that commitment ahead of their personal issues.

Likewise, we have seen instances where a husband and wife remarry because of the needs of the children. That is, it is in the best interest of the children to reside in a home where there is a Mom and Dad living together under the same roof as opposed to being shuffled from home to home. In theory, this sounds great. But before you consider this arrangement, consider whether it really is in the children's best interest. If what caused the two of you to separate in the first place was an unhealthy environment of screaming and testing each other, is it really in the kids best interest to subject them to this all over again.

MIKE'S STORY

Mike and Sue were married twelve years when they divorced. They had two children, a son age ten and a daughter who was eight. Though they were both exemplary parents always placing the needs of their children ahead of theirs, they conceded that they could not get along as husband and wife. Both were very driven, stubborn, and unable to compromise. He was always right and she was always wrong. As a result, they took out their frustrations in front of their children. One day, their daughter's teacher sent a note home. The girl had failed several tests and she had been an A student. She was wondering if something was going on in the house. Realizing that their nightly outburst was now affecting their children, they attempted counseling but when that failed, Sue filed for divorce.

As per the terms of the divorce, Mike had the children every other weekend. Both kids were heavily involved with sports and Mike coached soccer and little league. He also helped them with their homework as often as he could.

On their son's next birthday, Sue made a birthday party and invited Mike. After a long day of celebrating, she asked if he wanted to spend the night. The next morning, the children were all smiles at breakfast as they both commented how nice it was for Mom and Dad to be back together. Mike and Sue thought about what the kids said, and decided to resume seeing each other. After a few weeks, and a few more overnight stays, Mike moved back into the house. They remarried a year later and the problems that plagued Sue and Mike quickly resurfaced with Mike moving into a separate bedroom. After a short time, and seeing how this had a negative impact on the kids, Mike moved out.

♛ MARRYING YOUR EX BOYFRIEND

Similar to remarrying your Ex, proceed cautiously if you find yourself suddenly involved with an Ex boyfriend. Whether he was your high school sweetheart, the guy you dated throughout college, or your first relationship that you thought might bring you to the alter, the fact that you never got there before may be a clear sign that he may not be the one.

ANNETTE'S STORY

Annette was married fifteen years when she divorced her husband. Now single, she attended her twentieth high school reunion where she saw Gregg, her old boyfriend who she dated from her senior year and all through college. Gregg, too, was married and divorced.

They spent the evening talking about "old times." Coincidentally, though they had not seen or spoken to each other in over fifteen years, they lived within a half hour of each other. Feeling there was still some chemistry, they exchanged phone numbers which soon led to a dinner date. After less than six months, Annette suggested that since they already knew all there was to know about the other and they seemed to get along, why not take a chance and get married.

Gregg agreed and they were off to Vegas to exchange their vows. Within six months of saying I do, again, both Gregg and Annette were in our office pronouncing "they don't." They admitted that having the rings on their fingers created this feeling of involuntary servitude to each other. It was the same feeling they had that caused them to break up when they were in college.

♛ MARRYING YOUR BEST FRIEND

When a woman hears that you refer to your husband or wife as your best friend, she will smile and say something like, "That is so nice." It is very romantic to be referred to that way. But, as relationships develop through marriage, so does the title. Referring to your spouse as your best friend often means he/she is the person you most trust, the person you most want to be with, as well as the person you never want to be without.

If not married to, your best friend may also be that same person who you share your most intimate details about and the one to call when you need help. If that person is of the opposite sex, transitioning from being best friends to husband or wife comes with hidden surprises.

Accordingly, before you say I do, again, are you marrying someone who has always been in your life? Was he the guy who brought you soup when you were sick, drove you to the airport when you needed a ride, and would talk to you for hours on the phone about anything and everything? Is he your best friend? Sometimes, in the haste to get remarried, we sometimes choose someone who has always been there. But that does not mean he is now Mr. Right.

RONNIE'S STORY

Ronnie was recently divorced and credited her friendship with Larry for getting her through it. Ronnie and Larry met in law school, dated very briefly, but soon decided they were better off as friends.

During law school, the two studied together, shopped for clothes together, and even went to Vegas together though their relationship was platonic. They did date other people though they would discuss their relationships with each other.

When Ronnie met her husband to be, Larry was supportive. He was equally supportive when the marriage began to unravel. But after Ronnie's divorce, she thought she saw a different side of Larry. He was not involved with anyone and she pursued a romantic relationship which led to her re-marriage. Unfortunately after two years, that marriage also ended as they both realized they were both better off as friends and not lovers.

Ronnie admitted that she rushed to the altar. She thought that she already knew Larry and figured, "why not give it a chance." In retrospect, she should have gone by her original gut feeling that since there was not an original attraction, the passage of time did not change things. Furthermore, she was looking to remarry for the sake of being married and did not clearly think through why she was getting remarried.

☙ CAN YOUR SPOUSE REALLY BE YOUR BEST FRIEND?

It only seems logical that as a marriage develops, your spouse may become the person you trust the most, the person you most want to be with, and the person you never want to live without. But do not confuse the "best friend" whom you call when you need help or have concert tickets that you cannot use with the person you want to marry.

MISSY'S STORY

Missy was divorced for two years when she met Louis. He had never been married and had only a few guy friends. In a matter of weeks he pronounced his love for her though it took Missy a little longer to say the same. When she finally said I do, she referred to Louis as her best friend. She said they had become inseparable and he did everything for her. In fact, on Saturday mornings, Louis even accompanied Missy to the nail shop for her weekly pedicure.

Failing to make the distinction between being best friends and insecurity, Missy continued with her plans to walk down the aisle. However, within a few weeks of marriage, she felt as if she was choking. She now described her husband like a new puppy that was left alone as he waited for her to come home, called her ten times a day, could not make any plans without discussing it with her. One time when she was sick with the flu and they needed groceries, Louis couldn't even leave their apartment without her. Despite Missy's attempts to explain to Louis that she sometimes needed her freedom, he would not understand. After seeking marriage counseling to no avail, Missy filed for divorce.

☙ HE'S STILL MARRIED!!!!

Yes, love is blind. But it can also make you stupid. If you are seriously considering saying I do to someone who may still be married, this chapter should convince you to say I don't!

Getting seriously involved with someone who may still be married, and taking it to the level where you are talking about marriage after his divorce is finalized is not only dangerous but borders on being insane. Aside from the legalities that you cannot marry someone who is presently married, a person who is not divorced has not emotionally ended his relationship with his Ex. Despite what he says or what you think will be the result, you are in for an emotional rollercoaster ride that is guaranteed to make you ill.

LEGALLY SPEAKING! Even though parties may be separated for years, a person cannot remarry until the divorce becomes final. In most states, that process takes a minimum of six months and most likely longer as the clock does not start ticking until a petition for divorce is filed and the person initiating the process has served papers on her spouse.

☙ DATING THE MARRIED MAN

As discussed in Chapter One, statistics show that most people wait at least a year after a divorce before entering into a serious relationship. The majority of those who remarry do so within three years of the end of the first marriage.

During this transition period, it is probable that you will meet someone who has also separated from his spouse. There could be a natural attraction to this person as you have your past marriages in common. That alone, however, is no reason to rush the relationship. Instead, a man who is still married should set off an alarm louder than a parked car that has been compromised. Consider these warning signs:

- He says he is separated and his divorce will soon be final but he still wears his wedding ring.
- His online profile says that his divorce is pending.
- He says he is divorced but has not received his papers from the court.
- He says his Ex took care of everything.
- He still lives with his Ex but they have an understanding about seeing other people.
- He is uncomfortable to be seen with you in public and does(does not) always take your call.(calls)

☙ WHY ARE YOU ATTRACTED TO SOMEONE WHO IS STILL MARRIED?

What is it about married person that the opposite sex find attractive? Is it because someone else finds him desirable? Or is it exciting to be involved with someone who may not be legally divorced? When jogging my memory for a client who fell for a married man, I immediately recalled the following:

REBECCA'S STORY

I was practicing law less than five years when Rebecca contacted my office. She was in her forties, a striking blonde and had been divorced four years. She sought my services to annul her marriage from Tom as she found out that he was still married. I told her that the process was not difficult. Then she told me her story.

She was a flight attendant and met Tom on one of her flights. He would fly twice a month from Boston to Los Angeles on business. She said when they first met, he was extremely charming and she immediately accepted his offer to have dinner. He told her that his divorce was almost final and "the attorneys were finishing up the paperwork" to which she accepted this explanation.

Their relationship continued but was limited to Tom's twice a month trips to the West coast. After six months of dating, Rebecca did inquire again about Tom's divorce but she got the same explanation, only this time he added that he and his Ex needed to sell some assets so they could evenly divide their property.

A week before Christmas, Tom called Rebecca with good news. He said that his divorce was final and he could not wait to see her. He suggested that they meet in Las Vegas to celebrate his single status. She agreed and over dinner, he presented her with a diamond ring and asked to marry her. Rebecca immediately said yes and that night they went to a wedding chapel and tied the knot.

After their honeymoon in sin city, Tom told Rebecca that he still needed to live in Boston for about six months but would then move out to LA. She suggested that she could get a transfer to the East coast but he discouraged that. So they agreed to continue their twice a month bi coastal relationship.

One night while in LA, Rebecca received an alarming phone call. It was a female voice saying that she was Mrs. Chambers whom Rebecca assumed was the Ex wife. But the conversation that followed sent shockwaves down her spine. It turned out that Tom died of a heart attack while making love to his Ex who was not his Ex as they were still married. Yes it was true that they had filed for divorced but reconciled and cancelled the divorce proceedings.

Accordingly, before you say I do, again, insist on seeing written proof that a prior marriage has ended. Never accept his word that it's over!

♛ WHY DOES HE REALLY WANT TO MARRY YOU?

He has proposed and you are about to say I do, again. When you were in this position the first time around, chances are that your future was ahead of you. Concerns about money and children were probably not even a thought. Contemplating marriage for a second time requires that you are not only confident in your decision of whom to marry. You also need to place your fiancé under a microscope to make sure his reasons for marriage are as altruistic as yours. Consider the following:

Are you simply a tax deduction?

Jake's Story

Jake was forty-nine, never married, and enjoyed his independence. He was introduced to Jane by a mutual friend. She was married before with two sons who were attending college. In her property division agreement, she acquired the residence and within six months Jake gave up his apartment and moved in with Jane.

Jane admitted that her Ex took care of all the financial obligations and she was happy that Jake also assumed this role. From the moment she said "I do," her life with Jake became a walking spread sheet. Every penny they spent was calculated and itemized as he told her that being married gave them mutual tax benefits they did not enjoy when single. Though the house was in Jane's name, since Jake made the mortgage payment they were able to take the tax deductions for the interest paid.

Is he marrying you to get a green card?

Obtaining legal immigration status in this country is invaluable. As a result, persons have been known to marry solely to achieve this goal.

As a newly single person, you may become prey to someone seeking his green card disguised as your knight in shining armor. Sometimes in the rush to get remarried, you may get blinded by his romantic overtures and not see the warning signs.

Helen's story

Helen was thirty-three and divorced over two years when her friends told her it was time to find someone and get married again. In her quest to find Mr. Right, she had little success with introductions. Her brother-in-law then told her how his friend met his wife online. Helen decided to give it a try, paid a six month subscription, and created her profile.

Within hours she received messages from men who wanted to meet her. She was especially intrigued by one member. Brian's profile seemed to mirror hers. She also liked his photo and agreed to meet for a cup of coffee.

The first encounter went well and she commented how much she loved his British accent. A dinner date was set and soon thereafter she was in a committed relationship. It did not, however, bother her that Brian always was short of money as he explained that he had a very ill mother back home and was financially assisting her.

Within a month, Helen introduced Brian to her family and he quickly received their vote of confidence. Thereafter, Brian popped the question. Helen did say at first respond that she thought it was a little soon, but quickly changed her answer to yes. Brian also promised to buy her a ring that she would select after the wedding as he was expecting a settlement from an accident case. But for now, she proudly wore his aunt's ring that he inherited when she died.

Brian also said he wanted to pay for the wedding reception from his settlement money but suggested they get married by a Justice of the Peace now as he could not stand "to wait any longer." She agreed and on a Friday afternoon they met at the county clerk's office.

After thirty days of marriage, Helen inquired about Brian's settlement but accepted his answer that the attorneys were still working things out. Another two months passed and still no check. Brian then said that he needed to fly to England to visit his mother. Helen suggested that she go to meet the Mom but Brian was not enthusiastic about the idea and insisted they go again and make part of their trip their honeymoon.

While Brian was away, she discovered the business card of an attorney whom she assumed was handling the personal injury case. She called the office and then decided to call the attorney that Brian mentioned was handling his case. She announced to the receptionist that she was Brian's wife and was quickly told that his immigration petition was granted. Helen had been had. He used the marriage to gain immigration status and was never heard from again.

♛ DO YOU HOLD THE KEY TO HIS HEALTH INSURANCE?

If your fiancé appears too anxious to tie the knot, you are probably starting to question his motives. The following is a checklist of questions for the anxious fiancé.

- What are his motivations for wanting to get married?
- Does he need money?
- Is he always borrowing money from you?
- Is he being hounded by bill collectors?
- Is he financially dependent upon you?
- Does he have unresolved financial issues with his Ex?
- Is he involved in an ongoing case for child support or alimony?
- Has he had multiple short-term marriages?
- Does he have an ongoing criminal case that involves the repayment of money?
- Is he trying to put together some "deal" and needs money?
- Does he have tax liens or owe the IRS or any other governmental entity money?
- If he was not born in the United States, what is his immigration status?
     Is he a legal alien?
     Is he here on a work visa? Has it expired?
     Does he have a petition pending for a change in immigration status?

LEGALLY SPEAKING: A person who assists another in a fraudulent marriage is committing a criminal offense. The penalty for such crime may include a fine, jail time, or both.

See Chapter Nineteen for a discussion of obtaining credit information about your fiancé.

A Blue Print for a Successful Remarriage

Part two of this book prepares you to be emotionally, financially, and legally prepared before you say I do, again. The previous chapters in Part three will help you check his pulse, kick the tires, and make a thorough inspection both inside and out before you exchange your vows.

Before you walk down the aisle, the following material is provided for both of you and should be read together. It is your and your partner's blueprint for a successful remarriage.

Though I do not profess to be a marriage counselor or social worker, the role of an attorney often includes providing emotional support to your client. While you must always keep an objective mind, one would have to be totally insensitive to not show any care or concern for your client. As such, in conducting research for this book, I interviewed many individuals and couples of second marriages that worked out as well as failed second marriages. My research yielded the following results:

- *A successful remarriage requires that one or both spouses has moved past their divorce:*

Next to someone dying, the loss of a marriage can be one of the most emotionally trying experiences in one's lifetime. Regardless of fault, a divorce may represent shattered dreams and hopes as lives have been separated forever. For many, it takes a long time to accept that the person you once held hands at the altar with has now been taken away. When children are involved, their lives are changed forever. But to succeed a second time around requires that any grieving you have for your past relationship is complete and you are emotionally ready to move on.

- *A successful remarriage requires that the couple entering marriage understands the challenges of remarriage:*

Whether this is your first or subsequent marriage, every day of your marriage will not be as wonderful as your wedding day. There will be disputes, arguments, and fights. There will be times when you do not talk or kiss each other good night. But if you approach the marriage knowing there may be some bumps or hills or mountains to navigate, it will increase the chances for success.

- *Just because you are starting anew does not mean you have to discard the past:*

Whether one or both of you have had a prior marriage, you need to be open to ideas. There is no right or wrong way. Likewise, your former marriage should not be looked upon as "out with the old and with the new." You may like to work out at the gym after dinner or he may like to play poker with his friends on Thursday nights. Regardless, do not discard any routines or traditions.

- *Partners from a prior marriage do not carry forward resentment or hate toward their Ex:*

Dwelling on the past is not healthy for you or your new spouse. Furthermore, making sarcastic or mean-spirited comments about another's Ex may create resentment against you in the eyes of your new spouse.

- *When there are stepchildren, you need to establish your own relationship with a child and not play the role of a substitute teacher.*

Remember in school when you had a substitute teacher. Immediately I thought, Great, no homework and I can goof off. Substitute teachers are not given the same respect as the regular teacher. Likewise, children view stepparents the same way as you have to earn their respect. To do so, you must establish quickly that you are not a substitute and will never be a replacement for a parent. You are also not the enemy. Relationships with children that are not established early often lead to the biological parent siding with her child which ultimately can contribute to the breakdown of the marriage.

PRACTICAL POINT: Remarriage doesn't guarantee "happily ever after." Just like any marriage, a remarriage takes time, communication, and commitment. If children are involved, there are additional challenges, complications, and potential stresses that families must deal with. Successful remarried couples make sure they communicate well and show their love daily to each other, keeping their commitment fresh and strong. Rather than letting the things that irritate you get swept under the carpet, issues are addressed quickly and resolved.

♛ REMARRIAGE CAN BE MAGIC

In researching this book, I came across the following article. I thought the material was appropriate and its publisher has given permission for it to be republished.

Remarriage is tricky. Actually, marriage of any kind is tricky. To have a healthy marriage or remarriage, you need to develop many skills and have great determination to succeed.

Remarriage, though, has far more challenges than a first marriage. The good news, though, is that if you can get past those challenges, remarriage can be magic!

♛ HERE ARE FIVE WAYS YOU CAN CREATE A MAGICAL REMARRIAGE.

1. Remarriages often don't work because of all the baggage that the couple brings into the marriage with them. A person who has been divorced usually has more hurt, anger, and fear than a person who is getting married for the first time. A person, whose spouse has died, has grief and often guilt or anger to contend with. All of this emotion comes into the new marriage right along with the couple.

To have a great remarriage, you need to be aware of the baggage as you go into your new marriage, and you need to accept it. Awareness and acceptance combined have amazing powers to heal. Start with awareness and acceptance, and you can resolve old emotional issues to pave the way for a great remarriage.

2. Second marriages often include children from previous marriage or relationships. These children can cause problems in remarriage, but they don't have to. Although parenting someone else's child can be one of life's biggest challenges, it can be done. It can also be fun.

The trick is to know ahead of time, before the second marriage, how you're going to handle the logistics of joint parenting with an Ex. Include the children in this discussion. Be clear on what everyone's expectations are, know what the stepparent wants and can do, what the parent wants and can do, and what the children want and can do. When you lay out a family plan, you can create a wonderful blended family.

3. Ex spouses can be an obstacle to successful remarriage. If a previous divorce wasn't amiable, an Ex-spouse's resentment can create all kinds of problems for a second or third marriage. Ex spouses can file lawsuits accusing all kinds of manufactured crimes, they can demand money, and they can poison children with their hatred and anger.

To keep an Ex from ruining your second marriage, first, be sure you have the resources to have a good lawyer at your disposal. Second, make sure your new spouse knows what to expect from the Ex. Third, do everything possible to diffuse your Ex's anger. Don't engage in rehashing of your ended marriage. Avoid engaging in shouting matches with an Ex. Allow your Ex to feel what he or she feels and simply focus on dealing with whatever issue is at hand; leave old issues where they belong in the past. When you do all of this, you can leave your Ex spouse out of the picture and focus on a great remarriage.

4. To have a wonderful remarriage, you need to keep your focus on THIS marriage, not on past ones. When you've been married before, you have a benchmark of marriage in mind. If the last marriage was awful, that benchmark won't cause much problem.

If your previous marriage was good in any way, however, you might find yourself comparing your new spouse to your old spouse. Don't do this. Telling your new spouse, for example, that he isn't as good in bed as an Ex is a surefire way of killing a second marriage. Telling a spouse that he doesn't drive as well, cook as well, think as well, or do anything as well as a previous spouse dooms remarriage to failure.

5. Don't ever compare your current spouse to a previous one. In fact, you'll do best if you don't discuss a previous spouse at all unless you mention him or her in passing when sharing a memory of being someplace or doing something. To create a magical remarriage, think only about the remarriage.

Keep these tips in mind, and you can have a happy and successful, perhaps even magical, remarriage.

Republished with the permission of ARTICLEALLEY.COM
http://www.articlealley.com/article_91930_28.html

PART FOUR

COMPATIBILITY

MR. NEW VS. MR. OLD
HOW DO THEY COMPARE?

How compatible are you with your future spouse? Often in first marriages, we tend to overlook certain qualities in a rush to walk down the aisle. Perhaps our judgment becomes clouded and is overshadowed by the excitement of getting married.

For the second time around, you have already been there and do not want to make the same mistake twice. Accordingly, the following questions are designed for you to ask yourself about your fiancé. Score each response on a scale of 1 to 10 with 10 being the response most agrees with you. Then ask yourself the same questions about your Ex and compare your responses. You may be surprised that your fiancé shares many qualities that you disliked about your Ex.

1. **How comfortable is he with acts of public affection?**
2. **Is he secure about how he looks?**
3. **Is he secure about his age?**
4. **Is he secure about who he is?**
5. **Is he secure about his future (health, work, socially)?**
6. **Is he secure about his finances?**
7. **Does he have a good relationship with his family?**
8. **Does he show concern for others?**
9. **How close or far is he from your political beliefs?**
10. **Does he make you laugh?**
11. **Has he made you cry?**

12. Does he have a good sense of humor?
13. Does he make fun of you in a hurtful way?
14. Is he someone you could not live without?
15. If he weren't your fiancé, would you still be friends?
16. Does he enjoy just being with you?
17. Is he spontaneous?
18. Do you share many more interests than not?
19. Does he enjoy looking at you?
20. Has he ever expressed that he fantasizes about you?
21. Does he share the same spiritual and religious beliefs?
22. Does he take care of himself?
23. Do you feel safe being with him?
24. If he wasn't with you, would you set him up with your best friend?
25. Do you trust him to make health care decisions for you?
26. Does he avoid making unnecessary references to your age?
27. Does he enjoy your body?
28. Does he enjoy your mind?
29. Is he adventurous
30. Does he share similar intellectual values?
31. Does he have a similar approach to money and finance?
32. Does he recognize his own limitations?

APPENDIX A

PRE-NUPTIAL AGREEMENT

THIS AGREEMENT is made and entered into this ___ day of February, ____, by and between _____ of Orange County, California (hereinafter referred to as "Prospective Husband"), and _____, of Los Angeles County, California (hereinafter referred to as "Prospective Wife").

WITNESSETH:

A. WHEREAS, the aforesaid parties in contemplation and consideration of their forthcoming marriage desire to enter into a PRE-NUPTIAL Agreement; and

B. WHEREAS, the parties to this Agreement intend and desire to define that property which each party brings to the marriage, to the end that such property will be designated and set apart as the sole and separate property of the respective parties; and

C. WHEREAS, the parties to the Agreement have made to each other a full and complete disclosure of the nature, Extent, and probable value of all their property, estate and Expectancy; and

D. WHEREAS, the parties to this Agreement desire that neither of them shall be responsible for the debts of the other, which might have accumulated to the time of the signing of this Agreement, nor for any debts contracted hereafter unless both parties have agreed to assume the same; and

E. WHEREAS, neither Prospective Husband or Prospective Wife now has any right, title, claim or interest in or to the property, income or estate of the other by reason of their non marital relationship, or otherwise, and neither party is indebted to the other and both parties are in good health and are financially self-supporting; and

F. WHEREAS, this Agreement is entered into in consideration of marriage, and its effectiveness is Expressly conditioned on such marriage between the parties actually taking place; and if, for any reason, the marriage is not consummated, this Agreement will be of no force or effect; and

G. WHEREAS, both parties hereto recognize that this Agreement is a premarital agreement as defined in California Family Code section 1610 and understand and intend that the provisions of this Agreement shall prevail over the provisions of law applicable in the absence of this Agreement.

NOW THEREFORE, intending to be legally bound hereby and in contemplation and consideration, including, without limitation, the mutual promise, and agreements set forth herein and the completed marriage of the parties, the parties hereto agree as follows:

1. Effective Date: This Agreement shall be and become effective as of the date of the contemplated marriage between the parties, and its effectiveness is Expressly conditioned upon such marriage. If, for any reason, and irrespective of fault, the contemplated marriage does not take place, this Agreement will be of no force or effect.

2. Independent Counsel: The parties acknowledge and agree that they each have been represented by separate and independent legal counsel and have relied on counsel of their own choosing in negotiations for and in preparations of this Agreement. PROSPECTIVE HUSBAND warrants and represents that he is and has been represented by _____, Attorney at Law, and a member in good standing of the Bar of the State of California. PROSPECTIVE WIFE warrants and represents that he is and has been represented by _____, Attorney at Law, and a member in good standing of the Bar of the State of California. The parties acknowledge and agree that they have carefully read this Agreement, and that the provisions of the Agreement have been explained fully to them by their respective counsel.

3. Voluntary and Informed Consent: The parties further acknowledge and agree that they are fully aware of and understand the contents, legal effect, and consequences of this Agreement, and that they enter into this Agreement voluntarily, free from duress, fraud, undue influence, coercion or misrepresentation of any kind.

4. Property and Financial Disclosures

    a. The parties agree that, before Execution of this Agreement, a fair and reasonable disclosure of all of PROSPECTIVE HUSBAND'S property and financial obligations has been made by him to PROSPECTIVE WIFE, and a list of such property and financial obligations is set forth in Exhibit "A" attached hereto and incorporated herein by reference. It is understood that the figures and amounts of the property and financial obligations set forth in Exhibit "A" are approximate and not necessarily Exact, but they are intended to be reasonably accurate and are warranted to be the best estimates of such figures and amounts. PROSPECTIVE WIFE hereby expressly and voluntarily waives any right to disclosure of PROSPECTIVE HUSBAND'S property and financial obligations beyond the disclosure provided.

    b. The parties agree that, before Execution of this Agreement, a fair and reasonable disclosure of all of PROSPECTIVE WIFE'S property and financial obligations has been made by her to PROSPECTIVE HUSBAND, and a list of such property and financial obligations is set forth in Exhibit "B" attached hereto and incorporated herein by reference. It is understood that the figures and amounts of the property and financial obligations set forth in Exhibit "B" are approximate and not necessarily exact, but they are intended to be reasonably accurate and are warranted to be the best estimates of such figures and amounts. PROSPECTIVE HUSBAND hereby expressly and voluntarily waives any right to disclosure of PROSPECTIVE WIFE'S property and financial obligations beyond the disclosure provided.

    c. The parties agree that the foregoing disclosures are not an inducement to enter into this Agreement. PROSPECTIVE HUSBAND and PROSPECTIVE WIFE agree that each is willing to enter into this Agreement regardless of the nature or Extent of the present or future assets, liabilities, income, or Expenses of the other, and regardless of any financial agreements made for his or her benefit by the other.

5.   Rights Incident to Parties' Non marital Relationship:PROSPECTIVE HUSBAND and PROSPECTIVE WIFE acknowledge and agree that they have not previously entered into any other contract, understanding, or agreement, whether Express, implied in fact, or implied in law with respect to each other's property or earnings, wherever or however acquired or with respect to the support or maintenance of each other. Neither party now has, possesses or claims any right or interest whatsoever, in law or equality, under the laws of any state, in the present or future property, income or estate of the other, or a right to support, maintenance, or rehabilitation payments of any kind whatsoever from the other by reason of parties' non marital relationship. The parties acknowledge that they each have been advised by their respective counsel on California law respecting non marital relationships, and they each agree that neither has any rights and/or obligations arising out of their non marital relationship with each other.

6.   Separate Property Interests in Premarital and Post marital Assets and Acquisitions

   a.   PROSPECTIVE HUSBAND and PROSPECTIVE WIFE agree that all property, including the property set forth in Exhibit "A" belonging to PROSPECTIVE HUSBAND at the commencement of their contemplated marriage, and any property acquired by PROSPECTIVE HUSBAND during that marriage by gift, bequest, devise, or descent, shall be and remain his separate property. The parties further acknowledge and agree that any increase in the value of the PRE-NUPTIAL assets set forth in Exhibit "A", whether such increase in value is due to gain in market value, inflation, additional contribution by Prospective Husband or through the work product or efforts of Prospective Husband shall be and remain PROSPECTIVE HUSBAND'S separate property. The parties agree that change in the form of PROSPECTIVE HUSBAND'S assets as a result of the sale, Exchange, hypothecation, or other disposition of such assets, or a change in form of doing business shall not constitute any change of property characterization, and such assets shall remain PROSPECTIVE HUSBAND'S separate property regardless of any changes in form. PROSPECTIVE WIFE shall have no right, title interest, lien, or claim under the laws of any state in or to any of PROSPECTIVE HUSBAND'S separate property assets.

b.   PROSPECTIVE HUSBAND and PROSPECTIVE WIFE agree that all property, including the property set forth in Exhibit "B" belonging to PROSPECTIVE WIFE at the commencement of their contemplated marriage, and any property acquired by PROSPECTIVE WIFE during that marriage by gift, bequest, devise, or descent, shall be and remain her separate property. The parties further acknowledge and agree that any increase in the value of the PRE-NUPTIAL assets set forth in Exhibit "B", whether such increase in value is due to gain in market value, inflation, additional contribution by Prospective Wife or through

the work product or efforts of Prospective wife shall be and remain PROSPEC-
TIVE WIFE'S separate property. The parties agree that change in the form of
PROSPECTIVE WIFE'S assets as a result of the sale, Exchange, hypothecation,
or other disposition of such assets, or a change in form of doing business, shall not
constitute any change of property characterization, and such assets shall remain
PROSPECTIVE WIFE'S separate property regardless of any changes in form.
PROSPECTIVE HUSBAND shall have no right, title interest, lien, or claim under the
laws of any state in or to any of PROSPECTIVE WIFE'S separate property assets.

7.   Marital Efforts in Managing Each Party's Own Separate Property Interests

     a.   The parties acknowledge and agree that PROSPECTIVE HUSBAND
may devote considerable personal time, skill, service, industry and effort during
their marriage to the investment and management of his separate property and the
income thereof, specifically including, without limitation, PROSPECTIVE HUS-
BAND'S Existing or future orthopedic surgery practice. The parties acknowledge
and agree that even though the Expenditure of PROSPECTIVE HUSBAND'S
personal time, skill, service, industry and effort might constitute or create a community property interest, community property income, or community property
asset in the absence of this Agreement, no such community property interest,
income, or asset shall be created thereby , and any income, profits, accumulations,
appreciation and in increase in value of separate property of PROSPECTIVE
HUSBAND during the marriage shall be and remain entirely PROSPECTIVE
HUSBAND'S separate property.

     b.   The parties acknowledge and agree that PROSPECTIVE WIFE may
devote considerable personal time, skill, service, industry and effort during their
marriage to the investment and management of his separate property and the income thereof. The parties acknowledge and agree that even though the Expenditure of PROSPECTIVE WIFE'S personal time, skill, service, industry and effort
might constitute or create a community property interest, community property
income, or community property asset in the absence of this Agreement, no such
community property interest, income, or asset shall be created thereby, and any
income, profits, accumulations, appreciation and in increase in value of separate
property of PROSPECTIVE WIFE during the marriage shall be and remain
entirely PROSPECTIVE WIFE'S separate property.

8.   Marital Efforts in Managing the Other Party's Separate Property Interests:
The parties acknowledge and agree that during their marriage, one party may
choose to contribute considerable personal time, skill, service, industry and effort to the investment and management of the other party's separate property
and the income thereof. The parties acknowledge and agree that even though
any such contribution might constitute or create a community property interest,
community property income, or community property asset in the absence of this
Agreement, no such community property interest, income, or asset shall be created thereby. The parties further agree that any such contribution shall not create

any other claim, right, lien, or interest whatsoever, in favor of the party contributing the personal time, skill, service, industry and effort, in or to the other party's separate property and any income, profits, accumulations, appreciation and increase in value thereof during the parties' marriage.

9.   Separate Property Earnings, Deferred Compensation and Employee Benefits:The parties agree that any earnings, income or benefits, no matter their nature, kind or source, from and after the marriage, including but not limited to salary, bonuses, stock options, deferred compensation, and retirement benefits, shall be the separate property of the party earning or acquiring such earnings, income or benefits as though the contemplated marriage had never occurred. There shall be no allocation made of any such earnings, income or benefits between community property and separate property, and such earnings, income or benefits shall be entirely the separate property, and such earnings, income or benefits shall be entirely the separate property of the party earning or acquiring the same. The parties acknowledge their understanding that in the absence of this Agreement any earnings, income or benefits resulting firm the personal services, skills, industry and efforts of either party during the contemplated marriage would be community property.

10.   Separate Property Interests in Preexisting Retirement and Employment Benefit Plans:PROSPECTIVE HUSBAND presently owns a substantial beneficial interest in various retirement benefits, including, without limitation, a defined benefit pension plan. PROSPECTIVE WIFE acknowledges and agrees that pursuant to the terms of this agreement, all retirement benefits presently owned by or held for the benefit of PROSPECTIVE HUSBAND, together with any contributions, income, accumulations, appreciation and increase of such retirement benefits during the parties' marriage because of PROSPECTIVE HUSBAND'S personal services, skill, industry and efforts or otherwise, shall be and remain PROSPECTIVE HUSBAND'S separate property, and PROSPECTIVE WIFE shall have no right, title, claim or interest therein. The parties acknowledge their understanding that in the absence of this Agreement, contributions, income, accumulations, appreciation and increase of retirement benefits attributes to PROSPECTIVE HUSBAND'S personal services, skill, industry and efforts during the marriage would be community property.

PROSPECTIVE WIFE has been informed by her counsel and understands that pursuant to federal law, or the terms of PROSPECTIVE HUSBAND'S retirement benefit plan documentation, she may become entitled to rights and/or benefits in, to or from PROSPECTIVE HUSBAND'S a retirement benefits, including, without limitation, the right to a qualified joint and survivor annuity, or other death benefits. PROSPECTIVE WIFE hereby (a) waives all of her rights to receive any and all such benefits under any of PROSPECTIVE Husband's employment benefits; (b) consents to the designation by PROSPECTIVE HUSBAND of any person, persons or entity as beneficiary and to any change of beneficiary without further waiver or consent by PROSPECTIVE WIFE; (c) acknowledges her awareness of the effects of this waiver; and (d) agrees to Execute before a notary public all necessary waivers and consents requested by PROSPECTIVE HUSBAND after marriage, and within the particular time periods specified in the Internal Revenue Code, in order to effectuate the waivers herein.

11. Property Purchased with Borrowed Funds:PROSPECTIVE HUSBAND and PROSPECTIVE WIFE acknowledge that from time to time, either of them may obtain loans to purchase property or loans which are secured by property in which one of them may have an interest. The proceeds of any such loan shall be the borrower's separate property, notwithstanding that the lender may intend that repayment be made from income acquired during the marriage or from assets acquired during the marriage. Any property purchased with such borrowed funds and any property that secures a loan shall remain the borrower's separate property.

12. Waiver of Rights in Respective Estates: PROSPECTIVE HUSBAND and PROSPECTIVE WIFE agree that each party waives and relinquishes, to the fullest Extent lawfully possible, all right, title, claim, lien, or interest, whether actual, inchoate, vested or contingent, in law and equity, under the laws of any state or under federal law, in the other's property, income and estate by reason of proposed marriage, including without limitation, the following:

(a) All community property, quasi-community property, and quasi-marital property rights;

(b) The right to probate family allowance;

(c) The right to probate homestead;

(d) The rights or claims of dower, courtesy, or any statutory substitute now or hereafter provided under the laws of any state in which the parties may die domiciled or in which they may own real property;

(e) The right to inherit property from the other by intestate succession;

(f) The right to receive property that would pass from the decedent party by testamentary disposition in a will Executed before this agreement;

(g) The right of election to take against the will of the other;

(h) The right to take the statutory share of an omitted spouse;

(i) The right to be appointed as administrator of the deceased party's estate, or as Executor of the deceased party's will, unless appointed pursuant to a will Executed after the date hereof;

(j) The right to have Exempt property set aside;

(k) Any right created under federal law, including, without limitations, the Retirement Equity Act of 1984; and

(l) Any right, title, claim or interest in or to the property, income, or estate of the other by reason of the parties' non marital relationship.

13. Property Transfers Between Parties:The parties agree that nothing contained in this Agreement shall be constructed as a bar to either party's transferring, conveying, devising or bequeathing any property to the other. Neither party

intends by this Agreement to limit or restrict in any way the right to receive any such transfer, conveyance, devise or bequest from the other made after the parties' marriage. Neither party intends that by this Agreement either of them shall not be able to put the other party in control of their separate property or make a will in the other parties favor or name the other beneficiary of their separate property assets. However, the parties specifically agree that no promises of any kind have been made by either of them about any such gift, bequest, devise, conveyance or transfer from one to the other.

14. Management and Control of Separate Property Interests; Executing Arrangements:The parties agree that each party shall retain and enjoy sole and Exclusive management and control of his and her separate property, both during lifetime and upon death, as though unmarried. In order to accomplish the intent of this Agreement, each of the request of the other, his or her heirs, Executors, administrators, grantees, devisees or assigns, any and all such deeds, releases, as-signments or other instruments (including, but not limited to, the retirement plan waiver and consent form referred to in paragraph "10" of this Agreement), and such further assurances as may be reasonably required or requested to effect or evidence the release, waiver, relinquishment, or Extinguishments of the rights of the said party in the property, income or estate of the other under the provisions of this Agreement, and to assure that each party shall have sole and Exclusive management and control of his or her separate property.

15. Debt Obligations on Separate Property Interests. All obligations (including principal and interest) incurred due to or as a consequence of the purchase, en-cumbrance or hypothecation of the separate property of either party, whether real, personal or mixed, and all taxes, insurance premiums, and maintenance costs of said separate property, shall be paid from such party's separate property income or from such party's separate property funds, at such party's election, there being no community property by his terms of this Agreement. To the Extent that either party uses his or her separate property to pay the foregoing obligations of the other party, there shall be no right to reimbursement for such Expenditures.

16. Unsecured Debt Responsibility. All unsecured obligations of each party, no matter when incurred, shall remain the sole and separate obligations of each such party, and each party shall indemnify and hold the other harmless from liability therefore. Each party's unsecured obligations shall be paid from each respective party's separate property income or separate property funds, at such party's elec-tion, there being no community property by the terms of this Agreement. To the Extent that either party uses his or her separate property to pay the unsecured obligations of the other party, there shall be no right to reimbursement for such Expenditures.

17. Discharge of Living Expenses. The parties' join living Expenses shall be paid from a joint account to be established following the parties' marriage and into which each of the parties shall contribute their salaries from employment during

marriage. The term "joint living Expenses," as used in this paragraph, includes, but not limited to: food; household supplies; utilities; telephone, laundry; cleaning; clothing; medical and dental Expenses; medical, life, accident, and auto insurance; gasoline, oil and auto repairs; automobile purchases and/or lease payments; entertainment; support of any minor children that are the issue of the contemplated marriage; and joint gifts to third persons. The commingling of each party's separate property, and neither party shall acquire any right in the salary of the other by reason of such commingling.

18. Responsibility for Income Taxes, Effect of Joint Return: PROSPECTIVE WIFE shall pay the state and federal income taxes on her income, and shall indemnify and hold PROSPECTIVE HUSBAND free and harmless there from. PROSPECTIVE HUSBAND shall pay the state and federal income taxes on her income, and shall indemnify and hold PROSPECTIVE WIFE free and harmless there from. If the parties elect to file joint income tax returns, neither party shall be required to pay more income tax returns, neither party shall be required to pay more income taxes than he or she would have paid if he or she had filed a separate returns, gift tax returns, or other returns using a joint filling status shall not constitute any form of transmutation, or the creation of any community property or of any other rights or interest in contravention of this Agreement.

19. Support Liability: Nothing contained in this Agreement shall be construed as absolving either party of the statutory obligation to support the other during marriage or to affect in any way the obligation to support any children of the contemplated marriage. In the event of a separation or marriage dissolution, each party's obligation to support the other shall be determined and governed under the laws of the State of California.

20. Parties and Persons Bound: This Agreement shall bind the parties to the Agreement, and their respective heirs, Executors, administrators, representatives, assigns and any other successors in interest.

21. Voluntary Arms' Length Negotiations: The parties acknowledge and agree that this document is voluntarily entered into by and between them and that, as of the date of Execution of the Agreement, there is no confidential or fiduciary relationship Existing between them as defined under the laws of State of California. The parties further acknowledge that they have had Explained to each of them respectively, by their respective attorneys, the meaning of the terms "confidential relationship" and "fiduciary relationship." The parties specifically acknowledge that neither has ever offered business advise to the other, nor has either become dependent upon the other or relied on the other for advice, and that their relationship as of the date of Execution of this Agreement is a purely personal relationship of two engaged individuals intending to be married to each other at a future date.

22. Execution Formalities: The parties specifically agree that forthwith upon their Execution of the Agreement, their respective signatures shall be acknowledged by a notary public in their presence. The parties further acknowledge that the

date which is set forth on the first page of this Agreement is the actual date on which they and each of them are signing this Agreement. This Agreement or a memorandum of this Agreement may be recorded at any time and from time to time by either party in any place or office authorized by lay for the recording of documents affecting title to or ownership status of property, real or personal, specifically including, but not limited to, any county in which either party resides during the marriage and any county in which either party owns or may own real or personal property.

23. Applicable Law: This agreement is executed in the State of California and shall be subject to and interpreted under the laws of State of California.

24. Entire Agreement: This Agreement contains the entire understanding and agreement of the parties, and there have been no promises, representations, warranties, or undertakings by either party to the other, oral or written, of any character or nature, except as set forth herein.

25. Modification, Revocation: This Agreement may be altered, amended, modified or revoked only by an instrument in writing Expressly referring to this Agreement, Executed, signed and acknowledged by the parties hereto, and by no other means. Each of the parties waives the right to claim, contend, or assert in the future that this Agreement was modified, cancelled, superseded or changed by an oral agreement, course of conduct, or estoppel.

26. Invalidity, Severability: This Agreement has been jointly prepared and negotiated by counsel for each of the parties and shall bit be constructed against either party. If any term, provision, or condition of this Agreement is held by a court of competent jurisdiction to be invalid, void, or unenforceable, the remainder of the provisions shall remain in full force and effect and shall in no way be affected, impaired, or invalidated.

IN WITNESS WHEREOF, the parties have executed this Premarital Agreement on the date set forth on the first page of this Agreement.

DATED: _____   _____
                                PROSPECTIVE HUSBAND

DATED: _____   _____
                                PROSPECTIVE WIFE

DATED: _____   _____
                                ATTORNEY FOR

DATED: _____   _____
                                ATTORNEY FOR

WAIVER OF FURTHER DISCLOSURE

This Waiver of Further Disclosure is made and entered into this __ day of February, _____, in Orange County, California, by and between _____("PROSPECTIVE HUSBAND") and _____ ("PROSPECTIVE WIFE"), with references to the following facts and purposes:

A.   PROSPECTIVE HUSBAND and PROSPECTIVE WIFE, who are currently unmarried, plan to be married on _____.

B.   With the assistance of each party's separate and independent counsel, PROSPECTIVE HUSBAND and PROSPECTIVE WIFE are prepared to enter into a written premarital agreement. In the course of the negotiations for this premarital agreement, PROSPECTIVE HUSBAND has made disclosures of his property and financial obligations to PROSPECTIVE WIFE, and PROSPECTIVE WIFE has made disclosures of her property and financial obligations to PROSPECTIVE HUSBAND.

C.   PROSPECTIVE HUSBAND and PROSPECTIVE WIFE are each desirous of waiving any right to disclosures of property or financial obligations from the other party beyond the disclosures provided, and wish to make this mutual waiver of further disclosures prior to the Execution of their premarital agreement.

THEREFORE, for good and valuable consideration, including, without limitation, the mutual promises, conditions, and agreements set forth in the premarital agreement, and the contemplated marriage of the parties, the parties agree as follows:

1.   PROSPECTIVE HUSBAND hereby voluntarily, knowingly, and expressly waives any right to disclosures of the property and financial obligations of PROSPECTIVE WIFE beyond the disclosures provided by PROSPECTIVE WIFE up through and including the date of Execution of this document.

2.   PROSPECTIVE WIFE hereby voluntarily, knowingly, and expressly waives any right to disclosures of the property and financial obligations of PROSPECTIVE HUSBAND beyond the disclosures provided by PROSPECTIVE HUSBAND up through and including the date of Execution of this document.

3.   The parties acknowledge and agree that this document is Executed before Execution of the parties' premarital agreement, in accordance with the provisions of California Family Code § 1615 (a)(2)(b), even though the date of this document may be the same date as the date of Execution of the premarital agreement.

Dated:_____   _____
                            PROSPECTIVE HUSBAND

ATTORNEY'S CERTIFICATE FOR PROSPECTIVE HUSBAND

The undersigned hereby certifies that he/she is an attorney at law, duly licensed and admitted to practice in the State of California; that he/she has been employed by _____, PROSPECTIVE HUSBAND, a party to this Agreement, and that he/she has advised such party with respect to this Agreement and Explained to him the meaning and legal effect of it; and that said PROSPECTIVE HUSBAND, has acknowledged his full and complete understanding of the said Agreement and its said legal consequences, and has freely and voluntarily Executed the Agreement in my presence the ____ day of _____, _____.

_____
Print Name:

The above certificate is not applicable as I have voluntarily decided not to seek the advice of an attorney.

_____

Franklin M. Palmer

ATTORNEY'S CERTIFICATE FOR PROSPECTIVE WIFE

The undersigned hereby certifies that he/she is an attorney at law, duly licensed and admitted to practice in the State of California; that he/she has been employed by _____, PROSPECTIVE WIFE, a party to this Agreement, and that he/she has advised such party with respect to this Agreement and Explained to her the meaning and legal effect of it; and that said PROSPECTIVE WIFE, has acknowledged his full and complete understanding of the said Agreement and its said legal consequences, and has freely and voluntarily Executed the Agreement in my presence the ____ day of _____, _____.

_____
Attorney at Law

EXHIBIT "A"
ASSETS OF PROSPECTIVE HUSBAND
Listed below is the fair and reasonable disclosure of the property and/or financial obligations of the Prospective Husband:

EXHIBIT "B"
ASSETS OF PROSPECTIVE WIFE
Listed below is the fair and reasonable disclosure of the property and/or financial obligations of the Prospective Wife:

APPENDIX B

LAST WILL AND TESTAMENT

OF

_____

I, _____, a resident of _____ County, State of _____, declare this to be my Will and I hereby revoke all Wills and Codicils previously made by me.

FIRST: Family Status: I declare that I am married to, _____, and that I have _____ Child/Children by this marriage namely, _____, _____, and _____.

SECOND: Appointment of Executor:

I appoint _____ as Executor of this Will, to serve without bond. If the person named shall have predeceased me or should for any reason be unable or unwilling to serve as Executor, I appoint _____, as Executor of this Will, to serve without bond.

THIRD: Executor's Power:

I authorize my Executor to sell, at either public or private sale, any property belonging to my estate, either with or without notice, subject only to such confirmation as may be required by law, and to hold, manage and operate any such property.

FOURTH: Nomination of Guardian: If my child/children are, at time of death, and my spouse has predeceased me, then I hereby nominate _____ as Guardian of my child/children. If the Guardian named declines or is unable to act, or after appointment ceases to act as Guardian, then I do nominate _____ as Guardian of my Child/children.

FIFTH: Non Exercise of Power of Appointment. I hereby refrain from exercising any testamentary power of appointment that I may have at the time of my death.

SIXTH: Taxes. My Executor shall pay from the residue of my estate all inheritance, estate, and other death taxes (Excluding any additional tax that may be assessed under Internal Revenue Code Section 2032[a], including interest and penalties, that may, because of my death, be attributable to any assets properly inventoried in my probate estate).

The taxes shall be charged against my estate as though they were ordinary Expenses of administration without adjustment among the beneficiaries of my Will.

SEVENTH: I give, devise, and bequeath my entire estate as follows:

A.

B.

EIGHTH: Non Contest. Except as otherwise provided in this Will, I have inten-
tionally and with full knowledge omitted to provide for heirs. If any beneficiary
under this Will in any manner, directly or indirectly, contests this Will or any part
of it's provisions, any share or interest in my estate given to that contesting beneficiary under this Will is revoked and shall be disposed of in the same manner provided herein as if that contesting beneficiary had predeceased me without issue.

NINTH: Definitions: For the purpose of construing the terms of this Will;

A) Except when the context of this Will requires otherwise, the singular includes
the plural, and the masculine gender includes the feminine and neuter.

B) The terms "issue"; "child", and "children" include a person born out of wed-
lock if a parent-child relationship, as defined under the California Uniform Par-
entage Acts, Exists between this person and one through whom this person claims
benefits under this Will. These terms do not include persons who are adults at the
time of adoption.

C) For purpose of this Will, any beneficiary who dies within sixty (60) days after
my death, shall be deemed to have died before.

Executed this _____, day of _____, 200__ at _____ state of _____.

_____
Your name

On this date, _____ signed this document and declared it to
be his/her Will in our presence, and in the presence of each other, signed as wit-
nesses below. Each of us observed the signing of this Will by him/her and by each
other subscribing witness and knows that each signature is the true signature of
the person whose name was signed.

Each of us is a competent witness. We are acquainted with him/her, attest that
she/he is now more than eighteen (18) years of age. To the best of our knowledge,
he/she is of sound mind at this time and is not acting under duress, menace,
fraud, misrepresentation or undue influence.

Each of us declares under penalty of perjury under the laws of the state of California that the foregoing statement is true and correct, and that each of us signed below on this _____ of _____ 200__, at _____, state of _____.

                                              Address:
Signature: _____ _____
Print Name: _____ _____
                                              Address:
Signature: _____ _____
Print Name: _____ _____

APPENDIX C

ASSET ORGANIZER

LIST ALL NON-TAX DEFERRED ACCOUNTS (SAVINGS, CHECKING, CREDIT UNION, BROKERAGE, CD'S, TREASURY BILLS, OTHER)

NAME	VALUE	ACCOUNT #

LIST ALL TAX-DEFERRED ACCOUNTS (IRA, 401K, KEOGH, PENSION, PROFIT SHARING, KEOGHS, TAX DEFERRED ANNUITIES, OTHER)

NAME	VALUE	ACCOUNT #

LIST ALL INSURANCE BENEFITS (MILITARY, LIFE, HOME, DISABILTY, LONG TERM CARE, MEDICAL, AUTO, OTHER)

COMPANY   POLICY #   BENEFICIARY

_____   _____   _____

_____   _____   _____

_____   _____   _____

_____   _____   _____

FREQUENT FLYER MILES

Many frequent flyer programs allow you to transfer miles into your spouse and other family members. The airlines will require a copy of a death certificate and written documentation from you assigning the miles in your account. You can make written provision for the transfer in your Will or Trust.

NAME OF AIRLINE PROGRAM   ACCOUNT #   CUSTOMER SERVICE #

LIST ALLOBLIGATIONS (HOME, VACATION HOME, TIME SHARE, AUTOMOBILE, BOAT, MOTORCYCLE, RV LOANS, BANK CREDIT CARDS, DEPARTMENT STORES, OTHER)

NAME   ACCOUNT #   CUSTOMER SERVICE #

LIST ALLCHECKING ACCOUNT AUTOMATIC DEDUCTIONS (INTER-NET, CABLE, SATELLITE, CELL PHONE, NEWSPAPERS, INSURANCE, FITNESS CLUB AND OTHER MEMBERSHIPS)

NAME ACCOUNT #   CUSTOMER SERVICE #

_____ _____ _____

_____ _____ _____

_____ _____ _____

_____ _____ _____

_____ _____ _____

_____ _____ _____

_____ _____ _____